Contents

Plan Your Trip   4

Cancún (p49)
PASHU TA STUDIO/SHUTTERSTOCK ©

Welcome to Cancún & the Riviera Maya

With white-sand beaches, scenic ruins and fun-filled cenotes, this spectacular tourist corridor stretches 135km south from Cancún all the way down to Tulum. Whether traveling by car or bus, getting from one town to the next is a breeze – you can watch the sun rise over Isla Blanca, go diving in Parque Dos Ojos in the afternoon and still have time for a candlelit dinner in Tulum.

Paradise Beach, Tulum
SIMON DANNHAUER/SHUTTERSTOCK ©

Top Sights

Tulum Ruins

Maya ruins with astonishing views. **Tulum; p110**

PATRYK KOSMIDER/SHUTTERSTOCK ©

IREN KEY/SHUTTERSTOCK ©

Isla Blanca

One of Cancún's great secrets.
Cancún Centro; p34

Parque de las Palapas & Around

The heart of downtown Cancún.
Cancún Centro; p36

Plan Your Trip Top Sights

ROSARIENEBETANCOURT 9/ALAMY STOCK PHOTO ©

Museo Maya de Cancún & San Miguelito

Intriguing Maya ruins and artifacts. **Zona Hotelera; p52**

EGOROV/SHUTTERSTOCK ©

IMAGE BY THE STILLS. USED BY COURTESY OF MUSA ©

"Understanding" by Elier Amado Gil (Punta Ni~

Museo Subacuático de Arte

A unique underwater museum. **Zona Hotelera; p50**

Isla Mujeres Turtle Farm

Saving turtles one by one. **Isla Mujeres; p76**

Playa Norte

An unforgettable Caribbean seascape. **Isla Mujeres; p74**

Riviera Maya's Cenotes

Discover the Riviera's underground natural pools (cenotes). **Playa del Carmen; p92**

Diving Isla Cozumel

Diving and snorkeling island escape. **Isla Cozumel; p126**

Chichén Itzá

The Yucatán's best Maya site. **p66**

Laguna Bacalar

Secluded and wondrous crystal-clear lagoon. **p106**

Cobá

Home to the tallest pyramid in Quintana Roo. **p120**

Reserva de la Biosfera Sian Ka'an

Unesco-recognized and thriving biosphere. **p140**

LEFT: SAM CAMP/GETTY IMAGES © RIGHT: MADRUGADA VERDE/SHUTTERSTOCK ©

INSPIRED BY MAPS/SHUTTERSTOCK ©

Eating

Seafood is king along the coast, from fresh ceviche to fried whole fish and seasonal lobster. Yucatecan cuisine figures big on menus as well, including classics such as cochinita pibil (slow-cooked pork), salbutes (delightful fried tortilla snacks) and relleno negro (shredded-turkey stew). You'll also find Caribbean-inspired dishes.

Mother of Mexican Cuisine

Josefina Velázquez de León (1899–1968) is considered the mother of Mexican cuisine. She ran a successful culinary school and wrote more than 140 cookbooks, the most ambitious being *Platillos regionales de la República Mexicana*, considered the first book to collect Mexico's regional cuisine in one volume.

Chocolate

Archaeologists in the Yucatán have detected chocolate residue on plate fragments believed to be about 2500 years old, meaning the ancient Maya may have used it as a spice or cacao sauce similar to *mole*.

Frijol con Puerco

A regular weekly dish in many Yucatecan homes is *frijol con puerco*, a local version of pork and beans. Pork cooked with black beans is served with rice and garnished with radish, cilantro and onion.

Best Restaurants

Tempo Gourmet Basque cuisine created by 8-Michelin-star chef Martin Berasategui. Enough said. (p59)

Benazuza A tasting extravaganza of Mexican-inspired dishes. (p58)

Nixtamal Laguna Bacalar's slooow-food experience. (p107)

Hartwood Tulum's most popular restaurant blends fresh and local ingredients with international flavors and techniques. (p116)

Passion The French-Basque-inspired menu here was created by 8-Michelin-starred chef Martin Berasategui. (p100)

TONO BALAGUER/SHUTTERSTOCK ©

Best Seafood

Crab House Excellent stone crab, but fantastic shrimp dishes as well. (p59)

Javi's Cantina Serves seafood, choice beef cuts, chicken and various veggie options. (p84)

Puerto Santo Wood-fired whole fish is the specialty at this hidden oceanfront restaurant. (p42)

Best Tacos

Taquería Honorio Began as a hit street stall and features delicious tacos and *tortas*. (p116)

Best Cheap Eats in Cancún

Rooster Café Sunyaxchen Good little downtown breakfast spot to get some waffles and eggs Benedict. (p42)

Best Regional Restaurants in Cancún

Lonchería El Pocito Home-style Yucatecan cooking with great regional snacks. (p41)

La Habichuela Yucatecan tamales and main dishes drawing on ancient Maya recipes. (p42)

Where to Eat

Markets Produce; good, cheap eats.

Taquerías Tacos, *tortas* (sandwiches) and greasy delights.

Fondas Affordable, home-style meals.

Drinking & Nightlife

If you like to party you can get yourself into late-night mischief in Cancún, Playa del Carmen and Tulum. The islands of Isla Mujeres, Holbox and Cozumel have more of a subdued nightlife scene but you can always find cool drinking establishments that stay open past midnight. In some of the smaller towns it's pretty much last call at around 9pm.

Alcoholic Drinks

As elsewhere in Mexico, on the peninsula you will find the popular tequila and its cousin mezcal. Both spirits are distilled from the agave plant; one difference is that tequila comes from blue agave in the central state of Jalisco and is protected with Denomination of Origin status.

Cerveza (beer) is also widely available; the most popular mass-produced brew is Montejo. There is a growing number of breweries producing craft beers, such as Tulum, which makes a fine IPA, and Ceiba.

Balché is a Maya spirit that was offered to the gods during special ceremonies. It is fermented inside the hollow trunk of the *balché* tree with water and honey. *Balché* is not commercially available, but another Maya spirit, *xtabentún,* is easy to find in the region. *Xtabentún* is an anise-flavored liqueur that, when authentic, is made by fermenting honey.

Nightlife

People come to the region – with good reason – to enjoy incredible nightlife; the Yucatán can more than hold its own against Cabo, Vegas or anywhere else in the world. The big cities have just about everything: from clubs so loud the music pumps your heart for you to ritzy rooftop lounges to drag shows to funky dives. Outside of the biggest cities things are mellow. Rural nightlife is non-existent, unless

SUNSHINE PICS/ALAMY STOCK PHOTO ©

you count cats, dogs, roosters and the occasional marauding *coati*.

Best Nightlife

Amarula con Acento Tropical Somewhat hidden cocktail bar with DJs spinning house and tropical sounds. (p44)

Grand Mambocafé Downtown dance club featuring mostly Cuban salsa acts. (p45)

Nomads Cocina & Barra Artsy bar serving creative drinks and innovative Mexican cuisine. (p44)

Fusion Playa del Carmen's spot for live music, belly dancing and fire dancing. (p105)

Best Clubs

The City Latin America's largest nightclub features world-famous DJs and musicians. (p61)

Coco Bongo A Cancún institution with wild parties and acrobatic shows. (p63)

Papaya Playa Project Beachside Tulum club that hosts fabulous monthly full-moon parties and Saturday DJ nights. (p119)

Best Cocktail Bars

Amarula con Acento Tropical Trendy cocktail bar set in an old downtown Cancún house. (p44)

Nomads Cocina & Barra Creative drinks and innova-

tive cuisine draw the 'in crowd.' (p44)

Bar del Mar Zona Hotelera beach bar known for its habanero-infused Bloody Mary. (p62)

Best Local Bars

Las de Guanatos Locals dig the cool beers and spicy-hot sandwiches at this Guadalajara-themed bar. (p45)

Marakame Café Live bands jam at this pleasant open-air bar in a residential area. (p45)

Route 666 Bikers Bar Middle-class bikers and die-hard rockers bang their heads here. (p46)

Diving & Snorkeling

The Mexican Caribbean is world famous for its colorful coral reefs and translucent waters full of tropical fish so, not surprisingly, diving and snorkeling are the area's top activity draw. Add cenote (limestone sinkhole) dives to the mix and you truly have one of the most intriguing dive destinations on the planet.

Where to Snorkel

Many spots on the Yucatán's Caribbean side make for some fine snorkeling. The best sites are generally reached by boat, but areas near Isla Mujeres and Cozumel offer pretty decent beach-accessed spots. In Cozumel, you'll find some of the most popular snorkeling sites along the western shore. Inland you can snorkel in some of the Yucatán's famed cenotes. Some places rent gear, but, when in doubt, take your own.

Snorkeling with whale sharks has become very popular in recent years...too popular some might say. Just about all the dive shops on Isla Mujeres and Isla Holbox offer whale-shark tours. Just make sure before signing up that the tour operator abides by responsible practices recommended by the World Wildlife Fund. Keep in mind that tour operators can never fully guarantee that they'll actually track down a whale shark – sometimes nature has its own plans.

Where to Dive

Hands down Mexico's most popular scuba-diving location, Cozumel gets high praise for its excellent visibility and wide variety of marine life. The amazing sights are sure to keep even the most experienced diver in a constant state of awe.

With snorkeler-friendly shallow reefs, shark caves and an underwater sculpture museum, Isla Mujeres'

J.S. LAMY/SHUTTERSTOCK ©

sites appeal to both novice and advanced divers. From mid-May to mid-September you can snorkel with enormous whale sharks.

When to Go

Generally you can dive and snorkel year-round. But from November through January, the peninsula gets northerly winds and showers. In Cozumel they can blow so strongly that the harbormaster closes ports for days.

If you're visiting from June through November, keep an eye out for hurricane alerts. The best (if most crowded) time to see whale sharks is between mid-June and late August.

Best Cenotes for Diving

Parque Dos Ojos Belonging to one of the largest underwater cave systems in the world, divers have the unforgettable experience of exploring the mysteries of the deep at this cenote. (p93)

Cenote Angelita Wonderfully creepy waters capped by a foggy layer of hydrogen sulfide make branches of submerged trees seem all the more eerie. (p114)

Cenote Manatí Beautiful series of seven cenotes connected by a channel that winds through mangroves. (p116)

Gran Cenote Dive among small fish and see intriguing underwater formations in caverns. Dive shops in Tulum visit this site. (p115)

History

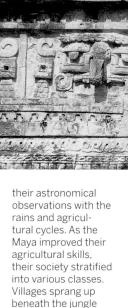

Reminders of the Yucatán's storied past are just about everywhere you turn on the peninsula: from extraordinary ancient Maya ruins and old-world cities to Caste War battleground sites. Even the relatively new kid on the block, the glitzy resort city of Cancún, has left an indelible mark on history as the region's cradle of mass tourism.

Beginnings

When cave divers near Tulum discovered the remains of a teenage girl's skeleton in 2007 they knew they had come across a huge find, but who would have thought at that time that the remains dated back 12,000 years? They spotted the ancient bones deep in an underwater pit at Sac Actun, which is connected to Parque Dos Ojos (p93) and makes up part of one of the world's largest underwater cave systems. Researchers believe that the young girl, who most likely fell into the cenote (sinkhole) and died there, is a descendant of ancient Siberians who crossed land (perhaps about 25,000 years ago) now submerged by the Bering Strait.

The Maya

Archaeologists believe Maya-speaking people first appeared in the Yucatán region around 2400 BC. Agriculture played an important role in their life. Watching the skies and noting the movements of the planets and stars, the Maya were able to correlate their astronomical observations with the rains and agricultural cycles. As the Maya improved their agricultural skills, their society stratified into various classes. Villages sprang up beneath the jungle canopy and temples were constructed from the abundant limestone.

As each successive leader had to have a bigger temple, larger platforms were placed upon earlier ones, forming gigantic step pyramids with a thatched shelter on top. In Quintana Roo,

RAFAL CICHAWA/SHUTTERSTOCK ©

the Maya built towns and cities from as far south as Kohunlich, which flourished from AD 600 to 900, all the way up to present-day Cancún, where small maritime communities thrived until the arrival of the Spanish conquistadors in the 16th century.

Maya Sites & Museums

Chichén Itzá One of the 'new seven wonders of the world.' Enough said. (p66; pictured)

Tulum Maya ruins perched atop a cliff with jaw-dropping views of the Caribbean blue down below. (p110)

Cobá A sprawling site in a jungle setting that's best explored on a bicycle, with the tallest pyramid in Quintana Roo. (p120)

Museo Maya de Cancún Fascinating Maya museum with hundreds of artifacts found in and around the peninsula. (p148)

San Miguelito Ruins of an ancient Maya maritime community, including an 8m high pyramid. (p52)

Zona Arqueológica El Rey The small structures here won't wow you like Chichén Itzá, but it's interesting nonetheless. (p56)

Maya Reads

For a concise but complete account of the ancient cultures of southern Mexico and Guatemala, read *The Maya* by Michael D Coe.

Shopping

HANNAMARIAH/SHUTTERSTOCK ©

Bargaining & Refunds

Prices for handicrafts sold in shops are generally non-negotiable, while in markets bargaining is the rule.

Refunds of a percentage of the 10% to 16% IVA tax on some purchases are available for tourists who arrive in Mexico by plane or cruise ship. Under the scheme, individual goods worth at least M$1200 (approximately US$63 at time of research) from participating stores qualify for the refund, on presentation of receipts with the shop's tax number (Registro Federal de Causantes) when the tourist leaves Mexico.

Best Places to Shop

Cancún Modern malls in the Zona Hotelera and old-school markets in downtown keep the shopping spree rolling. (p63 & p47)

Playa del Carmen The pedestrian walkway of Quinta Avenida (5 Av) is lined with stores and handicrafts stalls. (p91)

Isla Cozumel There's plenty of touristy garbage but there's also interesting stores if you look. (p125)

Best Stores in Cancún

La Isla Shopping Village Open-air center with a boutique stores section and an aquarium. (p64)

La Europea One of the best places in Cancún to stock up on top-shelf mezcal and tequila. (p63)

Mercado 23 Old-school downtown market where the locals do their shopping. (p47)

Guayaberas

Guayaberas – light, elegant shirts with four square pockets that are standard businesswear for men in southeast Mexico – originally hail from Yucatán.

Beaches

The Riviera Maya sits on prime beach real estate. Cancún was built as a resort city with its scenic beaches in mind, so the one constant is the fine white sands and turquoise waters. In Tulum, Maya ruins are perched atop a cliff above the beach, while in Isla Cozumel, a colorful reef awaits just offshore.

SWEDISHNOMAD.COM · ALEX W/SHUTTERSTOCK ©

Where to Beach-Bum

Along the Riviera Maya, you can't toss a coconut without hitting a gorgeous beach. Isla Mujeres' Playa Norte stands out for its incredibly calm and shallow cobalt waters, making it an ideal spot for swimming and kayaking. You'll also find very swimmable waters on the north side of Cancún's Zona Hotelera, while the remote Isla Blanca, further north, offers some of the city's quietest sands. In Tulum,

a gorgeous stretch of coast extends some 50km south from the city's famous ruins site all the way down to the jungle-backed sands of the Sian Ka'an Biosphere Reserve.

Best Beaches

Playa Norte Swimmable turquoise waters make this one of the finest beaches. (p74; pictured)

El Cielo Living up to its heavenly name, this lovely Cozumel beach is only accessible by boat. (p132)

Playa Garrafón Boasts some of the best snorkeling on Isla Mujeres and it's very reasonably priced. (p82)

Isla Blanca Escape from the busy hotel zone to this remote stretch of beach north of Cancún. (p34)

Best Beach Resort Destinations

Tulum The action shifts between a jungly hotel zone on the coast and an inland town jam-packed with bars and restaurants. (p109)

Isla Mujeres People get around in golf carts and scooters, or just walk: the downtown is only minutes from the beaches. (p73)

Cancún An oddball mix of glitzy hotel zone, local downtown scene and secluded beaches up north. (p49)

For Kids

BRETTCHARLTON/GETTYIMAGES ©

Snorkeling in caves, playing on the beach, running amok in the jungle... kids will find plenty of ways to keep busy in this region. And, as elsewhere in Mexico, children take center stage – with few exceptions, they're welcome at all kinds of hotels and in virtually every cafe and restaurant.

Getting Around

Car seats are compulsory for children under five, but if you'll be renting you may want to bring your own seat or booster from home, as agencies often add US$5 or even more per day to the cost of the car. Buses have comfortable seats, usually with onboard movies, and most (not all!) have bathrooms.

Kids can splash themselves silly in the Riviera at family-friendly beaches and cenotes. The area also has many theme parks if interest in the beaches starts to wane.

Best Destinations for Kids

Cobá Children dig the experience of bicycling through a thick jungle among the ancient ruins, while a series of nearby cenotes make for a fun afternoon swim. (p120)

Cancún From pirate-ship cruises and hotels with kids clubs to a wide offering of water-related activities and tours, boredom is simply not an option (especially if mom and dad are willing spenders) here. (p33)

Isla Mujeres With its shallow, swimmable beaches and a great little turtle farm, Isla Mujeres is a big hit with kids. (p73)

Best Animal Encounters

Isla Mujeres Turtle Farm Hundreds of sea turtles, both big and small, and there's an aquarium, too. The staff is very friendly and will take the time to explain how and why the farm protects the turtles. (p76)

Snorkel in the Caribbean Many beaches on the Yucatán's Caribbean coast provide calm waters and colorful marine life for beginners. (p129)

LGBTIQ

Cancún and the Riviera Maya are fairly broad-minded about sexuality. LGBTIQ travelers rarely attract open discrimination or violence, though it's still uncommon to see open same-sex affection in the smaller rural towns. Cancún has a small gay scene, and there are several gay-centric establishments around the region.

ALEXANDER_H_SCHULZ/GETTY IMAGES ©

The Law

Discrimination based on sexual orientation has been illegal since 1999 and can be punished with up to three years in prison.

Hotels & Restaurants

In general, LGBTIQ travelers will not have problems finding accommodations in Yucatán, nor do they have to seek out gay-friendly locales – any listing will welcome you.

Particularly in the Riviera Maya, LGBTIQ diners are common and dining with your same-sex spouse, partner or significant other will not cause heads to turn.

Gay-Friendly Mérida

A three-hour drive west from Cancún, gay-friendly Mérida hosts a primarily locals' LGBTIQ fiesta each July, with some 2000 to 3000 people attending.

Best LGBTIQ Entertainment

11:11 Cancún's top nightlife spot for LGBTIQ entertainment is a large house featuring drag shows and go-go dancers. DJs spin electronica and pop tunes till the sun comes up. (p46)

Playa 69 In Playa del Carmen, this gay dance club stages weekend drag-queen shows and has strippers from all over the world. (p103)

Four Perfect Days

Day 1

MARKOB85/SHUTTERSTOCK ©

Kick off the first day in the Zona Hotelera with some beach time at the lovely **Playa Gaviota Azul** (p57), or head just south for the enticing sands of nearby **Playa Chac-Mool** (p57). Have lunch at **Mocambo** (p60), then soak up some culture at the world-class **Museo Maya de Cancún** (p52), a museum holding one of the region's most important collections of Maya artifacts. Don't miss the ruins at the museum's adjoining archaeological site, **San Miguelito** (p52), or an afternoon visit to archaeological site **El Rey** (p56). Grab dinner at **Tempo** (p59) before making an appearance at **H Roof Nightclub** (p63) up above Harry's Steakhouse & Raw Bar for late-night DJ sets.

Day 2

AGE FOTOSTOCK/ALAMY STOCK PHOTO ©

Rent a car or scooter and wheel north from Cancún Centro to the remote beaches of **Isla Blanca** (p34; pictured). At the end of a bumpy dirt road you'll reach a gorgeous beach flanked by the Caribbean Sea to the east and a tranquil lagoon to the west. On the way back, procure fresh seafood at **Puerto Santo** (p42), then hang with the locals at **Plaza de Toros** (p40), a converted bullring building. Afterwards, hoof it to the **Bears Den** (p41) or **Peter's Restaurante** (p40), two of the Centro's finest restaurants, and cap off the evening with dancing at **Grand Mambocafé** (p45), a large venue with live bands playing Cuban salsa and other tropical styles.

Day 3

TONY PRISOVSKY/SHUTTERSTOCK ©

After two days in Cancún, make your way south to **Tulum** (p109; pictured) and its jaw-dropping coastal Maya ruins, which preside over a rugged coastline, a strip of brilliant beach and green-and-turquoise waters that'll leave you floored. Be sure to plunge into one of the numerous cenotes clearly marked from the highway. Return to the Zona Hotelera for the evening, ideally with a reservation at **Benazuza** (p58), at the Grand Oasis Sens hotel. More than just a meal, it's an experience as you feast on up to 30 gourmet courses. For a nightcap, drop by **La Destilería** (p61) to take in the lagoon view over margaritas.

Day 4

TONO BALAGUER/SHUTTERSTOCK ©

In Cancún, book a trip with Asterix to boat out to **Isla Contoy** (p44; pictured), an uninhabited island that's home to 170 bird species. It's a truly magnificent family-friendly trip that offers fun snorkeling, light hiking and lunch. You usually get back to the mainland around 6pm, and a delicious dinner awaits at **La Habichuela** (p42) or **El Tigre y El Toro** (p42), both located in Cancún Centro. During the summer lobster season, El Tigre y El Toro makes a popular pizza with the seafood topping. After dinner, swing by **Parque de las Palapas** (p37) and see what's happening on stage at the park's open-air cultural venue; there are often free concerts.

Need to Know

For detailed information, see Survival Guide p143

Currency
Peso (M$)

Languages
Spanish, Maya

Visas
All tourists must
have a tourist permit,
available on arrival.
Some nationalities also
need visas.

Money
Mexico is largely a cash
economy. ATMs and
exchange offices are
widely available. Credit
cards are accepted
in many midrange
and top-end hotels,
restaurants and stores.

Time
GMT/UTC minus five
(minus six for Chichén
Itzá)

Phones
Many US and Canadian
cellular carriers offer
Mexico roaming
deals. Mexican SIM
cards can be used in
unlocked phones; all
unlocked smartphones
are compatible with
Mexican data systems.

Daily Budget

Budget: Less than M$1000

Dorm bed: M$150–300

Double room in budget hotel: M$400–800

Street eats or economical set menu: M$20–100

City bus: M$4–12

Midrange: M$1000–1500

Double room in comfortable hotel: M$800–1600

Lunch or dinner in restaurant: M$100–200

Short taxi trip: M$20–50

Sightseeing, activities: M$100–250

Top End: More than M$1500

Double room in upscale hotel: from M$1600

Dining in fine restaurant: M$200–800

Car rental including liability insurance: per day from M$650

Tours: M$1000–2500

Useful Websites

Yucatán Today (www.yucatantoday.com) All things
Yucatán.

Yucatán Travel (www.yucatan.travel) Yucatán state
tourism site.

Loco Gringo (www.locogringo.com) Book homes and
hotels in Riviera Maya.

Lonely Planet (www.lonelyplanet.com/mexico) Destination
information, hotel bookings, traveler forum and more.

Riviera Maya (www.rivieramaya.com) Riviera Maya sights
and activities.

Maya Ka'an (www.mayakaan.travel) Great website with info
on tours and activities offered in Maya communities.

Arriving in Cancún & the Riviera Maya

✈ Cancún Airport

Frequent buses (M$82, 25 minutes) depart from the airport terminals to the bus station in Cancún Centro. For the Zona Hotelera, it's best to take an airport shuttle van (shared M$180, nonstop M$1100) or taxi (M$650) to your hotel.

✈ Cozumel International Airport

Shared shuttles from the airport into town cost about M$70. For hotels on the island's north and south ends, they charge M$150 to M$200.

🚌 ADO Bus Station

Buses arrive in Cancún Centro, where you can catch a bus or a taxi to your hotel, or walk if you're staying near the downtown terminal. Taxis waiting outside the bus station charge about M$150 to M$200 to the Zona Hotelera, depending on where you're going. Buses (M$12) to the hotel zone run along Avenida Tulum, adjacent to the ADO station.

Getting Around

Shared Van *Colectivos* are cheaper than buses. Most have frequent departures. They can get crammed and go rather rapidly, however.

Bus 1st- and 2nd-class buses go pretty much everywhere in the Yucatán.

Car Great option for traveling outside big cities. Expect to pay about M$750 a day for rental and gas.

Ferry Frequent boats depart from Playa del Carmen to Cozumel, Chiquilá to Isla Holbox and Cancún to Isla Mujeres.

Cancún & the Riviera Maya
Regions

Cancún Centro (p33)
Cancún's authentic heart features quiet stretches of soft-white sand, buzzing restaurant and bar zones and plenty of affordable accommodations.

Playa del Carmen (p91)
An ever-expanding tourist center that is quickly becoming one of the Riviera Maya's hottest destinations, with jam-packed beaches and a nonstop party.

Cobá ⊙

Cenote Azul ⊙⊙ Cristalino Cenote

Tulum (p109)
A dramatic stretch of postcard-perfect coastline paired with a bustling town center, surrounded by Maya ruins and cenotes.

⊙ Parque Dos Ojos

 Tulum Ruins

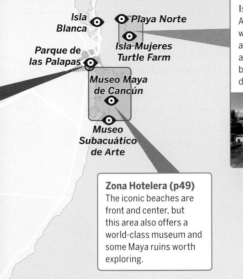

Isla Blanca

Playa Norte

Parque de las Palapas

Isla Mujeres Turtle Farm

Museo Maya de Cancún

Museo Subacuático de Arte

Isla Mujeres (p73)
A carefree sort of place, where folks still get around by golf cart and the crushed-coral beaches are an absolute dream.

Zona Hotelera (p49)
The iconic beaches are front and center, but this area also offers a world-class museum and some Maya ruins worth exploring.

Isla Cozumel (p125)
Relaxed and authentic neighborhoods exist alongside overrun, tourist-trappy corridors, but the real draw is the famed underwater environs.

Explore

Cancún
& the Riviera Maya

Tulum Ruins (p110) VLADIMIR KOROSTYSHEVSKIY/SHUTTERSTOCK ©

Explore ⊕

Cancún Centro

Some see Cancún Centro as the anti-Cancún, a sprawling, fast-paced city where tourism is certainly important but not the be-all and end-all. Most people stay in downtown for its affordable accommodations, but in recent years it has become a destination in its own right as a growing number of quality restaurants and bars crop up along the downtown streets.

The Short List

○ **Isla Blanca (p34)** Chilling on a white-sand beach flanked by the Caribbean Sea and a lagoon.

○ **Avenida Náder (p40)** Wining and dining at bars and restaurants in one of downtown's trendiest neighborhoods.

○ **Parque de las Palapas (p36)** Taking in a free concert outdoors while kids weave through the crowd in toy cars.

○ **Plaza de Toros (p40)** Drinking with locals at open-air bars and munching on snacks in a former bullring building.

○ **Parque Kabah (p40)** Taking a stroll along the park's trails and spotting herds of ring-tailed coatis.

Getting There & Around

🚌 Main routes are R-1, R-2 and R-27, all of which head to the Zona Hotelera. R-1 runs north along Avenida Tulum and will drop you at the Puerto Juárez Isla Mujeres ferry terminal. R-27 heads south along Avenida Tulum to Plaza Las Amé-ricas. Buses to the airport depart from the ADO station (M: B, D2; www.ado.com.mx; cnr Avs Uxmal & Tulum).

Cancún Centro Map on p38

Perlas (p40) EQROY/SHUTTERSTOCK ©

Top Sight 📷
Isla Blanca

◎ MAP P38, F1

parking M$50

...capists will love making *the trip* to Isla Blanca, ...g stretch of white sand *that* lies about 30km ...the city center. A dirt *road le*ads past swaths ...developed oceanfront, *offering* glimpses ...Cancún looked like be*fore* the 1970s ...ment boom. When you *rea*ch the end of ...you'll find a sublime be*ac*h sandwiched ...the ocean and a calm lag*o*on.

A Day at the Beach

Its isolated location at the untouched north-eastern tip of the Yucatán Peninsula means that Isla Blanca feels far from civilization but still offers a few amenities such as camping and tiny outdoor seafood restaurants. The main part of Isla Blanca is a narrow strip of sand separating the ocean on the eastern side from the lagoon on the western side. Walk north to find wilder virgin beach areas, or walk south to find quieter spots for beach lounging before reaching the northernmost resorts of Playa Mujeres.

Along the Way

Along the way to Isla Blanca make a stop at **Cabañas Playa Blanca** (📞cell 998-2139131; www.facebook.com/cabanasplayablancaislamujeres; beach club M$40, cabins M$800-1200; ⏰8am-6pm; 🅿), a little family-run beach club with rustic cabins for rent and a privileged beach affording views of Isla Mujeres. Stop for a few drinks before heading on to the beach.

Kitesurfing

Those seeking adventurous activities in remote locations might just love kitesurfing at Isla Blanca. The massive lagoon on the western side has calm shallow waters that are ideal for kitesurfing. You'll probably see dozens of kitesurfing sails fly above the lagoon whenever you go. There are quite a few kitesurfing outfitters that offer a variety of services to get you started, such as private beginner's courses for newbies or kite rental if you already have experience.

Getting There

Head north along Avenida Bonampak. Just past the Riu Dunamur hotel, the dirt road leads to Cabañas Playa Blanca and continues north until it dead-ends at the beach parking lot.

★ Top Tips

∘ You'll need to rent a car, as there is no public transportation to this beach.

∘ Driving down the potholed dirt road can be slow-going, but see it as an opportunity to soak up the scenery along the way.

∘ Watch out for potentially strong undercurrents when swimming.

✕ Take a Break

A beachside *palapa* sells drinks and snacks.

Cabañas Playa Blanca prepares fresh fish dishes and serves drinks.

Parque de las Palapas & Around

uch of the downtown social scene centers on
que de las Palapas and the lively surrounding
ts. The park sits on a large square with an
air concert venue and a row of food stands
orth end. Popular with Mexican families
e weekend concerts, cheap snacks and
mbience, the park is also a meeting point
s they prepare to hit the nearby bars
rants.

◎ MAP P38, D3

cnr Calle 2 & Tulipanes

Weekend Evenings in the Park

Tucked away in a neighborhood between two of downtown Cancún's main avenues, Parque de las Palapas is the main hub for local entertainment. The park comes alive on weekend evenings when families and groups of friends gather for the free, live entertainment and the city's most enticing street food. At the center of the park a main stage is set under a towering *palapa* roof, where you can expect to see anything from live jazz concerts to local beauty pageants. If you see a small crowd of locals in a circle, it's probably one of the Parque de las Palapas' iconic clown shows. Bordering the plaza vendors set up carts and sell a variety of handicrafts in addition to traditional Maya clothing.

Find Your Dessert

The eastern side of Parque de las Palapas is lined with bright neon food carts selling traditional Mexican street desserts. Instead of the famous *churros,* try the lesser-known marquesitas; these Yucatecan treats are crispy, rolled-up crepes filled with your choice of ingredients such as Nutella or Edam cheese.

Nightlife on Avenida Náder

After meeting at Parque de las Palapas, many locals will head two blocks east, across Avenida Tulum, to an up-and-coming area of trendy nightspots along Avenida Náder. With cocktail bars spinning house music and stylish restaurants serving contemporary Mexican cuisine, this is about as cool as downtown gets. Meanwhile, east of Palapas, there are sidewalk eateries staging live cover bands and boisterous bars catering to a mostly local clientele.

Getting There

Any R-1, R-2 or R-27 bus from the Zona Hotelera will drop you in the neighborhood.

★ **Top Tips**

o Things tend to get going a bit later at the bars along Avenida Náder, the strip just east of Avenida Tulum.

o While on the square watch out for euphoric children behind the wheels of battery-operated toy cars (pictured).

✗ **Take a Break**

Feeling snacky? Grab a bite at the **Mexican food stalls** (Margaritas; mains M$20-50; ⏲7:30am-midnight) at the square's north end, where you'll also find street vendors selling refreshing *tejuino* (fermented corn drink with ice and lime) and f... made ice cre...

Nearby, No... Cocina &... (p44) r... al spo... off a... wh...

Cancún Centro

Isla 10 6
Blanca

Av José García de la Torre

Naranja
Cereza

Av Bonampak

Av Uxmal
12

11
17

16

Avenida
1 Náder

Av Náder

Av Náder

E

Av José García de la Torre

Tierra
7

City
Tourism
Office

27

Avenida
1 Náder

5

Av Tulum

ADO Bus
Terminal

Av Tulum

Av Tulum

Avenida
Tulum

Claveles

Azucenas

Margaritas

Tulipanes

Parque de
las Palapas 21

Alcatraces

Av Cobá

Flamboyan

Flamboyan

Chaca

Laurel

Margaritas

Gladiolas

Orquídeas

13

24

D

Av Chichén Itzá

Palmera
Robie

Laurel
Palmera

Jazmines
Rosas

Av Yaxchilán

Punta Allen

Nicchehabí

23

Av Uxmal

Robie

Punta
Conoco

14

Punta
Yoquen

Av Sunyaxchén

Tauch

Av Xel-Ha

Av Tankah

alle 31

Av Chichén Itzá

Amigos de
Isla Contoy

26

Av Tankah

Av Yaxchilán

Av Las
Playas

Av Palenque

15

3

4

Cancún Centro

For reviews see

◉ Top Sights p34
◉ Sights p40
⊗ Eating p40
⊗ Drinking p44
🏠 Shopping p47

F   E   D   C

Av Cobá
4

5

6

7

8

Av Cobá

Av Xcaret

Av Xcaret

Av Xcaret

Av Cobá

Av La Costa

Av Tankah

Av Palenque

Av Yaxchilán

Av Mayapán

Av Nizuc

Av Xpuhil

Av Contoy

Av Labná

Av Acanceh

Av Nichupté

Av Kabah

Av Tulum

Av Sayil

Av Bonampak

Jaleb
Tejón
Pecarí
Pecarí
Nube
Cielo
Cielo
Tierra
Tierra
Mar
Fuego
Lluvia
Lluvia
Agua
Agua
Viento
Viento
Brisa
Nube

Plaza de Toros

Plaza Las Américas

⊗ 22
⊗ 19
◉ 18
⊗ 3
⊗ 9
20
8 ⊗
7
🏠 25

Sights

Avenida Náder   STREET

1 ⊙ MAP P38, E4

This avenue one block east of Avenida Tulum has emerged as one of the Centro's top restaurant and bar zones.

Parque Kabah   PARK

2 ⊙ MAP P38, B8

Beloved by local nature-lovers and fitness-lovers alike, this jungle park in the city remains mostly untouched. Runners and walkers flock to the 1.9km dirt trail bordered by lush jungle, athletes work out at the outdoor gym, and kids climb on the sizable wood playground. As you explore, you'll probably spot some local Cancún wildlife, such as coatis. (cnr Avs Kabah & Nichupté; admission free; ⏱sunrise-sunset)

⚊za de Toros   LANDMARK

⚊AP P38, F6

⚊ the Plaza de Toros are ⚊s, some with music, ⚊argely local crowd. ⚊s Bonampak & Sayil)

⚊as   BEACH

⚊reat kids'
⚊ and free
⚊cess
⚊n. (Av

Avenida Tulum   AREA

5 ⊙ MAP P38, E3

Cancún's main north–south thoroughfare is Avenida Tulum, a wide boulevard lined with banks, shopping centers and restaurants.

All Ritmo   WATER PARK

6 ⊙ MAP P38, F1

Little ones can splish and splash to their heart's content at this water park, which also has mini-golf and shuffleboard. The turnoff is 2km north of the Ultramar ferry terminal. 'Punta Sam' *colectivos* on Avenida Tulum (opposite the bus terminal) will drop you at the turnoff, and it's a short walk from there. (☎998-881-79-00; www. allritmocancun.com/servicios; Puerto Juárez-Punta Sam Hwy Km 1.5; adult M$320-350, child 5-12yr M$270-290; ⏱10am-5pm Wed-Mon)

Eating

Peter's Restaurante   INTERNATIONAL $$$

7 ✕ MAP P38, F4

Set on one of downtown Cancún's busiest avenues, Peter's Restaurante has a homey charm and some of the best cooking in the city. Dutch chef Peter Houben has blended European, Mexican and international cuisine, with beautifully prepared dishes such as the mushroom ravioli appetizer and fresh salmon fillet in lemon sauce with a spicy hint of *chile de àrbol* (tree chili). (☎998-251-93-10; www.

facebook.com/peterscancun; Av Bonampak 71, btwn Calles Sierra & Robalo;
dinner M$375-655; ⊙6-10pm Tue-Sat)

Bears Den INTERNATIONAL $$$

8 ✖ MAP P38, F7

In this casual, open-air restaurant
on the 2nd floor of a shopping
center, Quebec native Christopher
Vallieres prepares exquisitely re-
fined dishes like tender pork belly
with sake-and-pear purée and
seared tuna with mango-jalapeño
chutney and soy-ginger glaze. The
dining area catches a nice lagoon
breeze and service is spot-on.
(☑998-688-67-43; www.thebears
dencancun.com; 2nd fl, Plaza Azuna,
Av Sayil; mains M$220-460; ⊙3-11pm
Tue-Sun)

Lonchería El Pocito YUCATECAN $$

9 ✖ MAP P38, B1

For authentic Yucatecan home-
cooking, locals often recommend
this fan-cooled *palapa* restaurant
and it's easy to take an instant lik-
ing to the place. The changing daily
menu features savory regional
classics like *queso relleno* (stuffed
cheese), *papadzules* (diced egg
enchiladas) and *relleno negro
de pavo* (stewed turkey). Wash
it down with a refreshing *agua
de chaya* (Mexican tree-spinach
water). (☑998-252-26-54; Calle 31
Norte, btwn Calles 10 & 12; tacos M$16-
17, mains M$120-130; ⊙8am-10pm
Mon-Fri, to 8pm Sat)

Papadzules (diced egg enchiladas)

MATTHEW CLEMENTE/GETTY IMAGES ©

Puerto Santo

SEAFOOD $$$

10 MAP P38, F1

In a gated residential community about 500m south of the Puerto Juárez ferry terminal, this hidden oceanfront restaurant wins over locals with dishes like chili-sautéed octopus *tostadas,* fresh ceviche and wood-fired whole fish. To get here, leave an ID with a security officer at the Puerta del Mar entrance. (WhatsApp only 998-845-28-52; www.facebook.com/puertosantocancun; Residencial Puerta del Mar Supermanzana 84, Puerto Juárez; appetizers M$85-189, mains M$179-320; 1-11pm; P ♠)

El Tigre y El Toro

ITALIAN $$

11 MAP P38, E3

Gourmet thin-crust pizza and homemade pastas are served in a candlelit gravel garden at El Tigre y El Toro ('tiger' and 'bull' are the owners' nicknames). Many locals rank this as Cancún's *numero uno* izza joint. The seasonal lobster ping comes highly recommend- 998-898-00-41; www.facebook. igreyeltoro; Av Náder 64; mains ?05; 6pm-12:30am Mon-Sat, n Sun; ♠ ⌖; R-1, R-2)

o

INTERNATIONAL $$

?

d by strings of moonlight, staurant sits walled patio

on downtown Cancún's central Avenida Uxmal. The main menu boasts artisanal creations made primarily with local organic ingredients, and the daily specials wall always has tempting culinary surprises and inventive cocktails to try. (998-884-17-41; www.facebook. com/lafondadelzancudo; Av Uxmal 23; mains M$135-285; 7pm-midnight Mon-Sat; ♠; R-1)

La Habichuela

FUSION $$$

13 MAP P38, D3

This elegant restaurant has a lovely courtyard dining area, just off Parque de las Palapas. The specialty is the *cocobichuela* (shrimp and lobster in curry sauce served inside a coconut with tropical fruit), but almost anything on the menu is delicious. The menu even has a Maya-English dictionary! (998-884-31-58; www.lahabichuela. com; Margaritas 25; mains M$215-470, cocobichuela M$650; 1pm-midnight; P ♠; R-1)

Rooster Café Sunyaxchen

CAFE $

14 MAP P38, C3

A main go-to cafe for locals in search of a place to write, work or hang out, this trendy coffee shop has a central location, close to Market 28. Try items such as Monte Cristo waffles and homemade breads from the breakfast menu, or stop by in the afternoon for desserts, salads, burgers and *paninis.* (998-310-46-92; Av Sun-

Before it Was Cancún

Cancún was inhabited long before developers came along in 1970 with plans to build a glitzy resort city. As you'll see at the Zona Hotelera's archaeological sites of San Miguelito and El Rey, Maya communities flourished in the area from 1250 to 1550. Despite the relatively small size of the community when compared to, say, Chichén Itzá or Cobá, the settlement played an important role in regional maritime trade and fishing. Archaeologists believe that by around 1550 the arrival of the Spanish conquistadors forced the settlers to flee their prime beachfront property and it remained mostly abandoned after that.

Fast forward about 400 years. After much debate about where to build Mexico's next big resort destination, Mexico's tourism honchos agreed in 1970 to embark on a mass development project on an island sand spit shaped like the number 7. The name of the place was Cancún. At that time, the remote land was known as Isla Cancún (Cancún Island) and it overlooked a tiny fishing village called Puerto Juárez, just across the bay. Puerto Juárez is now home to the busy Isla Mujeres ferry terminals. Once development was underway, vast sums of money were sunk into landscaping and infrastructure, yielding straight, well-paved roads, potable tap water and great swaths of sandy beach. As the hotel zone mushroomed, Cancún Centro cropped up on the mainland and became one of the fastest growing cities in Mexico – today it's Quintana Roo's most populated city and economic capital.

yaxchen s/n, Plaza Sunyaxchén; mains M$75-160; ⏰7am-11pm; 📶)

Tacos Rigo   TACOS $

15 ❌ MAP P38, A4

There's a taco joint on nearly every block in Cancún, but this one has been a local favorite for more than 30 years. One bite of the *al pastor* (spit-roasted pork) taco and you'll understand why. (📞998-884-49-65; cnr Avs Las Playas & Palenque; tacos M$15-29; ⏰8am-midnight)

Kotaro   RAMEN $

16 ❌ MAP P38, E3

Tucked away in an alley off the trendy Avenida Náder, this tiny Japanese restaurant is beloved for its delicious noodles and (dumplings). Start with or spicy edamame acc by an order of sake, th a rock shrimp *bao* w sauce, followed by one of Kotaro's ra

Parque Nacional Isla Contoy

Spectacular Isla Contoy is a bird-lover's delight: an uninhabited national park and sanctuary that is an easy day trip from Cancún or Isla Mujeres. About 800m at its widest point and more than 8.5km long, it has dense foliage that provides ideal shelter for more than 170 bird species, including brown pelicans, olive cormorants, turkey birds, brown boobies and frigates, and is also a good place to see red flamingos, snowy egrets and white herons.

Whale sharks are often sighted north of Contoy between June and September. In an effort to preserve the park's pristine natural areas, only 200 visitors are allowed access each day. Bring binoculars, mosquito repellent and sunblock. Guided tours to Isla Contoy give you several hours of free time to explore the island's interpretive trails, climb a 27m-high observation tower and get in a little snorkeling.

Amigos de Isla Contoy (Map p38, B3; 998-884-74-83; www. facebook.com/amigosdeislacontoyac; Local 1, 2nd fl, Plaza Bonita Mall; 9am-5pm Mon-Fri) has detailed information on the island's ecology.
Asterix Tours (998-886-42-70; www.contoytours.com; Calle Vialidad s/n, V&V Marina; adult/child 5-12yr US$117/102; tours 9am-5:30pm Tue-Sun) runs trips, as do operators on Isla Mujeres.

(998-217-75-17; www.facebook.com/kotaroramen; Av Náder 104; bao M$40-55, ramen M$90-170; 2-11pm on-Sat, to 7pm Sun; ❄)

rinking

rula con
Tropical COCKTAIL BAR

d from the street only by a
nd neon sign, Amarula
p38, E3) blends dark,
ith the architectural
d Cancún house.
nu far outshines
e signature drinks
name ('with
ing classic
like jamaica

(hibiscus flower), regional fruits and chili peppers.

DJs spin house, jazz and tropical sounds. (cell 998-3325680; www. facebook.com/amarulaconacento tropical; Av Náder 104; 9pm-3:30am Wed-Sat; R-1)

Nomads Cocina
& Barra COCKTAIL BAR

17 MAP P38, E3

Showing off with an artsy vibe where geometric tiles meet concrete and brick, Nomads draws Cancún's young 'in crowd' with creative cocktails and innovative Mexican cuisine. The indoor area allows friends to sit down to a late dinner (mains M$125 to M$220), while the back area under the stars is standing room only. (📞998-898-31-92; www.nomadscancun.com; cnr Av Náder & Mero; 🕐6pm-2am Tue-Sun; 🚌R-1)

Marakame Café   BAR

18 🚇 MAP P38, D8

An excellent open-air breakfast and lunch spot by day, and a popular bar with live music by night. The bartenders, or mixologists if you will, prepare martinis and mango margaritas, and they do mimosas for Saturday and Sunday brunch (M$238). It's a short taxi ride from downtown. (📞998-887-10-10; www.marakamecafe.com; Av Circuito Copán 19, near Av Nichupté; 🕐8am-1am Mon-Fri, 9am-2am Sat, 9am-midnight Sun; 📶; 🚌R-27)

Grand Mambocafé   CLUB

19 🚇 MAP P38, C5

The large floor at this happening club is the perfect place to practice those Latin dance steps you've been working on. Live groups play Cuban salsa and other tropical styles. (📞998-884-45-36; www.facebook.com/grandmambo cafecancunoficial; 2nd fl, Plaza Hong Kong, cnr Avs Xcaret & Tankah; cover M$60-180; 🕐9:30pm-3am Wed-Sat; 🚌R-2)

Las de Guanatos   BAR

This indoor-outdoor space at Plaza de Toros (see 3 🔘 Map p38, F6) has

Frigate bird at Parque Nacional Isla Contoy

earned fame over the years for its massive 1L *micheladas,* a Mexican drink made with beer, lime juice, sauces and more, usually rimmed with sweet-and-spicy chili powder. For a midnight snack, try the *torta ahogada* (a yummy pork sandwich drowned in mild or super-hot salsa) – ask for the spicy sauce on the side. (📞998-892-95-56; www.facebook.com/guanatostoros; Av Bonampak s/n; 🕑11am-3:30am Tue-Sun, from 1pm Mon)

Black Pub
PUB

20 🔲 MAP P38, F7

Imitating the vibe of a stylish British pub, this bar attracts everyone from local university students to 50-somethings. It's the live late-night bands playing classic Mexican and US rock songs that have the crowd singing along and raising their beers. (📞998-267-74-09; www.facebook.com/theblackpub; cnr Avs Bonampak & Sayil; 🕑2pm-3am Tue-Sat; 🛜)

11:11
GAY

21 🔲 MAP P38, D3

The main room in this large house stages drag shows, go-go dancers and the like, while DJs in smaller rooms spin electronica and pop tunes till the sun comes up. Look for the black and rainbow design outside. (Once Once; 📞cell 998-1352243; www.1111gayclubcancun.com; Claveles s/n; 🕑10pm-6am Fri-Sun; 🚃R-1)

Route 666 Bikers Bar
BAR

22 🔲 MAP P38, D5

Lining a downtown street with motorcycles and a small crowd every weekend, Route 666 is an open-air bar catering to rockers and middle-class bikers. Live tribute bands sing English- and Spanish-language covers of rock groups, from Molotov and Caifanes to Mötley Crüe and Aerosmith. You'll find plenty of regulars here, mostly locals in search of beer, chicken wings and bands. (📞cell 998-2658625; www.facebook.com/route666bikersbar; Av Yaxchilán 100; 🕑7pm-3am Sun-Wed, to 4am Thu, to 5am Fri & Sat)

Underground Find

Local musicians and artists gather at **Mora Mora** (Map p38, A2; 📞cell 998-3007080; www.facebook.com/mora mora-1434309116861854; Av nque 10, btwn Av Chichén Itzá e 6 Poniente; 🕑5pm-1am t), a muralled under-venue, which operates urant and gallery as rear garden, you're h Mexican hip-metal acts grind-' sets. Definitely u're looking n's youth

La Taberna de los Amigos
SPORTS BAR

23 🟢 MAP P38, D2

A popular bar and grill with pool tables, televised matches and a sports book in the back for die-hard gamblers. (📞998-887-54-33; www.lataberna.com.mx; Av Yaxchilán 23; ⊙noon-3am; 🛜)

La Chopería
BAR

This bar at Plaza de Toros (see 3 ◎ Map p38, F6) draws a crowd, as much for the draft beer as the icy air-con. (📞998-140-74-70; www.facebook.com/ lachoperiadecancun; Av Bonampak s/n; ⊙noon-6am; 🛜)

Shopping

Mercado 23
MARKET

24 🔒 MAP P38, D1

This market is a nice reality check if you're tired of seeing the same old tourist knickknacks elsewhere. (www.facebook.com/mercado23 cancun; Jabín 9; ⊙8am-7pm; 🚃R-1)

Plaza Las Américas
MALL

25 🔒 MAP P38, E7

Plaza Las Américas, at the south edge of the centro, is a vast modern shopping mall that includes department stores, a multiplex cinema and a food court. Don't confuse it with Plaza América, a small, aging arcade on Avenida Cobá with a few airline offices. (Av Tulum 260; ⊙10am-10pm)

Mercado 28
SHOPPING CENTRE

26 🔒 MAP P38, B3

Locals head to Mercado 28 for clothes, shoes, inexpensive food stalls, crafts and so on. (Mercado Veintiocho; 📞998-892-43-03; www. facebook.com/mercado28cancun mexico; cnr Avs Xel-Há & Sunyaxchén; ⊙8am-7pm)

Mercado Municipal Ki-Huic
MARKET

27 🔒 MAP P38, E4

This warren of stalls and shops carries a wide variety of souvenirs and handicrafts. (Av Tulum s/n; ⊙9:30am-9pm; 🚃R-1)

Explore

Zona Hotelera

Spanning 19km along an L-shaped island flanked by Laguna Nichupté to the west and the Caribbean Sea to the east, the Zona Hotelera boasts some remarkable seascapes, along with touristy high-rise hotels and loud nightclubs lining the main strip. The white-sand beaches get top billing here and you can visit a world-class museum and its adjoining Maya ruins.

The Short List

∘ **Museo Subacuático de Arte (p50)** *Snorkeling in the shallow waters of a unique underwater museum featuring submerged sculptures.*

∘ **Museo Maya de Cancún (p52)** *Wandering a world-class museum, home to impressive Maya artifacts.*

∘ **Scuba Cancún (p56)** *Taking the plunge into the ocean or a cenote with one of the city's most experienced dive shops.*

∘ **Playa Langosta (p57)** *Swimming in some of the calmest waters of the Zona Hotelera and relaxing on the beach's powdery sand.*

Getting There & Away

🚌 To reach the Zona Hotelera from Cancún Centro, catch any bus with 'R-1,' 'Hoteles' or 'Zona Hotelera' displayed on the windshield as it travels along Avenida Tulum toward Avenida Cobá then eastward on Avenida Cobá. South of Avenida Cobá, along Avenida Tulum, you can also catch the 'R-27' to the Zona Hotelera.

🚕 From the airport you're best off taking a shared shuttle van or taxi.

Zona Hotelera Map on p54

"Blessings" by Elier Amado Gil (Punta Sam Gallery)

Top Sight 📷
Museo Subacuático de Arte

British-born sculptor Jason deCaires Taylor, along with five sculptors, launched a unique underwater museum in 2010 off the coasts of Cancún and Isla Mujeres to divert divers away from deteriorating coral reefs. With some 500 life-sized sculptures it's one of the largest underwater art attractions in the world.

◎ MAP P54, C8

MUSA Underwater Museum

☎998-849-52-26

www.musamexico.org

snorkeling tour US$42, 1-tank dive US$65

Environmental Considerations

The Museo Subacuático de Arte (also known by its initials MUSA) was constructed with environmental purposes in mind: to create a whole new artificial reef structure for the area's diverse marine life to colonize. The permanent, large-scale sculptures are firmly fastened to the seabed and made from pH-neutral cement to promote coral life; the figures were made with holes to provide shelter for small marine wildlife.

Three Galleries

The museum has been divided into three underwater galleries: **Salon Manchones** off the coast of Isla Mujeres, with a depth of 8m that makes it ideal for scuba diving; **Salon Nizuc** off the southern tip of Cancún, with a 4m depth that is best suited for snorkeling tours; and the small **Punta Sam Gallery** for snorkeling just north of Cancún. At Salon Manchones, some 450 human statues comprising the Silent Revolution exhibit were modeled after locals from the Mexican fishing community where deCaires Taylor lives.

For Kids

If you're with kids who are too young to snorkel or dive, you can try a glass-bottom boat tour to see the sculptures without entering the water.

Artists in Collaboration

The project began with English sculptor Jason deCaires Taylor, who blended his skills in sculpting as well as diving and underwater photography to create an awe-inspiring underwater world. The five other artists who have contributed to the museum over the years are: Mexico artist Karen Salinas Martinez, Mexican artist and president of the museum Roberto Diaz m, Rodrigo Quiñones Reyes, industrial- pecialist Salvador Quiroz Ennis and ulptor Elier Amado Gil.

★ Top Tips

o The shallower Salon Nizuc site allows snorkeling only; divers must go to the Isla Mujeres gallery instead.

o When booking a tour ask if the US$12 'docking fee' is included in the price.

o Aquaworld (p57) visits both the Salon Nizuc and Isla Mujeres sites, whereas Scuba Cancún (p56) only goes to the Isla Mujeres gallery.

✗ Take a Break

The small marina at Scuba Cancún has a snack shop on a terrace with a lovely lagoon view. After an outing with Aquaworld head over to waterfront Harry's Steakhouse & Raw Bar (p59) for fresh seafood and house-aged steaks.

★ Getting There

MUSA sits just off the coast. Make arrangements with a dive shop; Scuba Cancún is a good one.

Top Sight 📷

Museo Maya de Cancún & San Miguelito

After hurricanes forced the city to shut down its former anthropology museum in 2004, the shiny new Museo Maya de Cancún opened its doors in 2012 with hurricane-resistant, reinforced glass. It came at a time when Cancún, a city known more for its white-sand beaches and unabashed party scene, sorely needed a cultural offering. And culture it got, with a museum showcasing more than 400 Maya artifacts found at key sites around the Yucatán Peninsula.

◎ MAP P54, D5

Maya Museum

☏ 998-885-38-43

www.facebook.com/
museomayacancun

Blvd Kukulcán Km 16

adult/child under 1
M$70/free

🕐 9am-6pm Tu

Museo Maya de Cancún

The beautifully contemporary Museo Maya (Spanish for Maya Museum) sits at the entrance to San Miguelito, and boasts several galleries displaying artifacts discovered at different Maya archaeological sites throughout southeastern Mexico and other areas of Central America.

San Miguelito

The price of admission to the museum includes access to the adjoining ruins of San Miguelito (p58), an archaeological site that has preserved the vestiges of an ancient Maya trade city. Wide dirt paths on the 80-hectare site lead through the jungle to remains of houses, a palace with 17 columns, a temple and an 8m-high pyramid, which has been rebuilt three times.

Maya History

While the archaeological site of San Miguelito is currently named after the old coconut ranch that operated here in the middle of the twentieth century, its history as a city actually began more than 800 years ago. From AD 1200 to AD 1550, Maya settlements thrived throughout much of Cancún, and San Miguelito was once the most important, reaching about two miles long and including the nearby site now called El Rey. The city was accessible from both the ocean and Nichupte Lagoon, making it a strategic port where many trade ships had to stop. The architecture in San Miguelito follows the east coast style found at Tulum, Xcaret and Xel-Ha, leading archaeologists to believe that ~e four cities had strong ties to one another. ~haeologists also believe that San Miguelito ~ very prosperous and well visited, since its ~ngs show that they had been renovated ~ times over the years. It fell into disrepair ~rty and was eventually abandoned ~ after the Spanish conquest of Mexico ~ middle of the 16th century.

★ **Top Tips**

○ To avoid crowds, get to the museum between 9am and 11am or during the lunch hour from 2pm to 4pm.

○ Bring insect repellent for strolling in the lush gardens of the San Miguelito archaeological site, especially for late-afternoon visits.

○ The museum has free parking but the small lot fills up fast during peak visiting hours (after 11am).

○ No need to wear sneakers. The pathways are cleared and level, and visitors aren't allowed to climb the structures, so you'll be just fine in your favorite vacation sandals.

✖ **Take a Break**

Grab some cold drinks and chill on the soft sands of **Playa Delfines** (Blvd Kukulcán Km 17.5; P), just south of the museum.

★ **Getting There**

Take a R-1, R-2 or R-27 bus to Blvd Kukulcán Km 16.5.

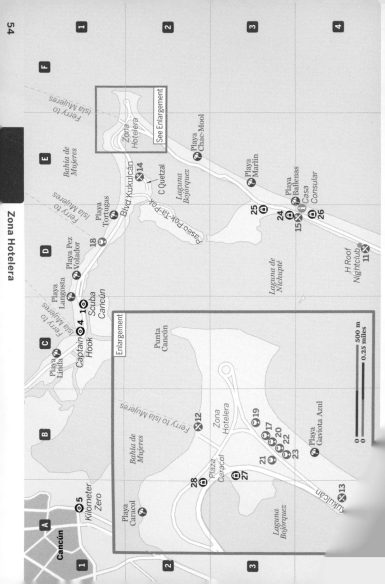

Cancún

Kilometer Zero

Playa Caracol

Bahía de Mujeres

Ferry to Isla Mujeres

Plaza Caracol

Zona Hotelera

Punta Cancún

Laguna Bojórquez

Playa Gaviota Azul

Kukulcán

Enlargement

Playa Linda

Ferry to Isla Mujeres

Playa Langosta

Scuba Cancún

Captain Hook

Playa Pez Volador

Playa Tortugas

Ferry to Isla Mujeres

Bahía de Mujeres

Blvd Kukulcán

C Quetzal

Zona Hotelera

See Enlargement

Ferry to Isla Mujeres

Paseo Pok-Ta-Pok

Laguna Bojórquez

Laguna de Nichupté

Playa Chac-Mool

Playa Marlin

Playa Ballenas

Casa Consular

H Roof Nightclub

0   500 m
0   0.25 miles

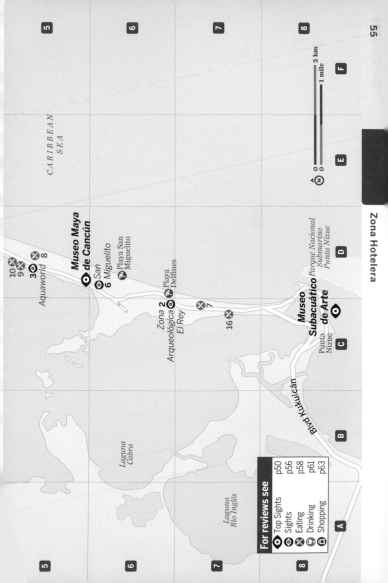

Zona Hotelera

Museo Maya de Cancún

Aquaworld

10
9
3
8

San
6 Miguelito

Playa San
Miguelito

CARIBBEAN
SEA

Zona 2
Arqueológica
El Rey

Playa
Delfines

7

16

**Museo
Subacuático
de Arte**

Parque Nacional
Submarino
Punta Nizuc

Punta
Nizuc

Laguna
Cabra

Laguna
Río Inglés

Blvd Kukulcán

N

0   1 mile
0   2 km

A   B   C   D   E   F

For reviews see	
Top Sights	p50
Sights	p56
Eating	p58
Drinking	p61
Shopping	p63

5   6   7   8

Sights

Scuba Cancún   DIVING

1 ◉ MAP P54, C1

A family-owned and PADI-certified dive operation with many years of experience, Scuba Cancún was the city's first dive shop. It offers a variety of snorkeling, fishing and diving expeditions (including cenote and night dives). It also runs snorkeling and diving trips to the Museo Subacuático de Arte (p50), as well as whale shark outings. (☏998-849-52-25; www.scubacancun.com.mx; Blvd Kukulcán Km 5.2; 1-/2-tank dives US$62/77; ◷7am-8pm Mon-Sat, from 8am Sun)

Zona Arqueológica El Rey   ARCHAEOLOGICAL SITE

2 ◉ MAP P54, C6

In the Zona Arqueológica El Rey, on the west side of Blvd Kukulcán, there's a small temple and several ceremonial platforms. The site gets its name from a sculpture excavated here of a noble, possibly a *rey* (king), wearing an elaborate headdress. El Rey, which flourished from AD 1200 to 1500, and nearby San Miguelito were communities dedicated to maritime trade and fishing. (www.inah.gob.mx; Blvd Kukulcán Km 18; M$55; ◷8am-4:30pm; ᵫR-1, R-2)

Zona Arqueológica El Rey

Zona Hotelera's Top Beaches

Playa Langosta (Map p54, D1; Blvd Kukulcán Km 5) In the middle of the north end of Zona Hotelera, Playa Langosta is a gem of a place for swimming. Facing Bahía de Mujeres, the beach is coated with Cancún's signature powdered coral sand and the waters are quite shallow, making it good for snorkeling. Once you've had enough of the water there are lots of beach restaurants and bars.

Playa Gaviota Azul (Map p54, B4; Blvd Kukulcán Km 9) A beautiful little curve at the end of the bay, mostly monopolized by beach clubs. Access is from the north side of Coco bongo's (p63).

Playa Chac-Mool (Map p54, E2; Blvd Kukulcán Km 9.5) With no parking, this is one of the quieter beaches in Cancún and there's usually a lifeguard on duty. There's no food, but there are stores and restaurants near the access, opposite Señor Frogs.

Aquaworld   TOURS

3 ◉ MAP P54, D5

Runs a hybrid submarine/glass-bottom boat out to the Museo Subacuático de Arte (p50), an underwater museum with hundreds of submerged life-sized sculptures. This tour is a good option for kids or non-swimmers, as opposed to the snorkeling tours that go out to the site. (📞998-689-10-13; www.aquaworld.com.mx; Blvd Kukulcán Km 15.3; adult/child 4-11yr US$47/24; ⏰7am-8pm)

Captain Hook   BOATING

◉ MAP P54, C1

...re's nothing like a swashbuck-...adventure with sword fights ...annon battles to get kids' ...ations running wild. This ... tour aboard a Spanish ...eplica includes dinner ser-

vice, and it costs a pretty doubloon if you go for the steak and lobster option. On the other hand, kids cost only US$5 if they eat strictly from the buffet bar.

Boats depart from Marina Capitán Hook. Parking is available in the lot across the bridge. (📞998-849-44-53; www.capitanhook.com; Blvd Kukulcán Km 5, Marina Capitán Hook; adult US$84-109, child 2-12yr US$5-56; ⏰tour 7-10:30pm; 👪)

Kilometer Zero   LANDMARK

5 ◉ MAP P54, A1

A favorite spot for Cancún athletes. Set where the Zona Hotelera meets Cancún Centro, Kilometer Zero has a lush green outdoor gym in the middle of the boulevard, as well as a family-friendly area across the road with a playground, workout area and lockers. The famous Cancún Ciclopista also

FOTOS593/SHUTTERSTOCK ©

Blvd Kukulcán at night

begins here: a 9km path for jogging, walking, cycling and roller-blading. (cnr Blvd Kukulcán & Av Bonampak; admission free; 🚌R-1)

San Miguelito ARCHAEOLOGICAL SITE

6 ◎ MAP P54, D6

This archaeological site (p52) contains more than a dozen restored Maya structures inhabited between AD 1200 and 1550, prior to the arrival of the conquistadors. It is underwhelming if compared to some of the nearby ruins in Tulum or Cobá, but a nice cultural diversion if you're staying in Cancún. A path from the Museo Maya de Cancún leads to remains of houses, a palace with 17 columns and the site's tallest structure: the 8m-high Pirámide (Pyramid),

which was rebuilt three times. Access to the ruins is included in the entrance fee to the Museo Maya de Cancún (p52). (📞998-885-38-43; www.facebook.com/museomaya cancun; Blvd Kukulcán Km 16.5; 🕘9am-5:30pm; 🚌R-1)

Eating

Benazuza MEXICAN $$$

7 🍴 MAP P54, C7

Up to 30 courses of surprising molecular cuisine. The dining experience at contemporary restaurant Benazuza incorporates traditional Mexican-inspir dishes like tacos and chilis tha have been transformed into n shapes, flavors and textures cutting-edge cooking techn

The price here includes molecular cocktails at the bar, all dinner courses, and desserts unlike any you've ever tried. (📞998-891-50 00; www.facebook.com/restaurante benazuza; Blvd Kukulcán Km 19.5, Grand Oasis Sens Resort; per person $1376; ⏰7-10pm Mon-Sat; 🚌R-1)

Tempo BASQUE $$$

8 🍴 MAP P54, D5

Dazzling contemporary elegance and impeccable service characterize Tempo, but it's the nine-course tasting menu of elaborate gourmet Basque cuisine with a molecular touch that has made this restaurant one of the best in Cancún. Created by 8-Michelin-star chef Martin Berasategui, Tempo provides an experience where each course delights and surprises the palate, from flavorful seafood recipes to lavish desserts. (📞998-881-17-90; www.tempocancun. com; Blvd Kukulcán Km 16.5, Paradisus Cancun Resort; mains M$555-875, 9-course tasting menu M$1762; ⏰6-11pm; 🚌R-1)

Crab House SEAFOOD $$$

9 🍴 MAP P54, D5

Offering a lovely view of the lagoon that complements the seafood, the long menu here includes many shrimp and fish-fillet dishes. Stone crab is the specialty, which (along with lobster) is priced by the pound. Both are served from crystal-clear tanks. The establishment prides itself on having no holidays: not even for hurricanes.

(📞998-193-03-50; www.crabhouse cancun.com; Blvd Kukulcán Km 14.7; mains M$420-1150; ⏰noon-11:30pm; 🅿🛜; 🚌R-1)

Fred's House SEAFOOD $$$

10 🍴 MAP P54, D5

One of Cancún's most beautiful restaurants, Fred's House features warm contemporary style and tropical gardens by Nichupté Lagoon. At this seafood eatery, you can order oysters from the raw bar, or try the popular wood-grilled octopus and several lobster dishes. For perfect sunsets or a special occasion, call in advance to reserve one of the waterfront dining pavilions. (Seafood & Oyster Bar; 📞998-840-64-66; www.fredshouserestaurant.com; Blvd Kukulcán Km 14.5; mains M$325-850; ⏰1pm-midnight; 🚌R-1)

Harry's Steakhouse & Raw Bar STEAK $$$

11 🍴 MAP P54, D4

Stunning, renowned Harry's serves house-aged steaks, plus super-fresh fish and a famous cotton-candy treat. The architecture's impressive too, with indoor waterfalls, plenty of decking over the lagoon and two bars – one indoors and one out. Service is impeccable. Try the jungle-theme lounge or the new exclusive roof nightclub upstairs, and don't miss peeking at the tequila mezcal display. Yum! (📞998-840-65-50; www.harrys.com.mx; Blvd Kukulcán Km 14.2; mains M$410-1290; ⏰1pm-1am; 🚌R-1, R-2)

Off the Map: Alternative Tourism on the Rise

A growing number of alternative-tourism outfits are reconnecting people with Yucatecan culture. Hooking up with a community-based tour not only allows you to tap into that culture but it also provides support for local economies.

Many Maya communities, for instance, are welcoming tourism – a great way to help maintain their language and culture. Maya Ka'an (www.mayakaan.travel) supports ecotourism in numerous communities throughout the state, including lagoon tours in Muyil, just south of Tulum, which can easily be visited on a day trip from Cancún. Other Maya Ka'an tours teach ancient Maya medicine and healing practices. Another good source of information on sustainable tourism is website www.caminossagrados.org.

North of Cancún, on the road to Isla Holbox (p64), an ecotourism center called **El Corchal** (📱cell 998-1657105; pepecorcho05@gmail.com; Av Hidalgo s/n, Solferino; tour per person M$700) runs interesting tours in the seldom-visited town of **Solferino**. Nature enthusiasts will enjoy the center's kayaking and jungle camping trips. Even if you have no time for the tour, you should definitely make it a point to stop in Solferino and check out the town's magnificent orchid garden and its famous 700-year-old sacred Ceiba tree. Solferino lies about 125km northwest of Cancún and just 15km south of Chiquilá, from where you can catch ferry boats to Isla Holbox.

Mocambo

SEAFOOD $$$

12 🍽 MAP P54, B2

Definitely one of the best seafood spots in the Zona Hotelera, the *palapa*-covered Mocambo sits right on Playa Caracol and serves up excellent dishes such as whole *mero* (grouper) and a savory seafood paella. A trio plays Mexican classics from 3pm to 5pm. It's past Hertz down a narrow alley that leads to the beach. (📱998-883-05-88; www.mocambocancun.mx; Blvd Kukulcán Km 9.5; mains M$265-550; ⏱noon-11pm; 🅿 🛜; 🚌R-1)

Restaurante Natura

VEGETARIAN $$

13 🍽 MAP P54, A4

This little bistro offers up a good mix of natural and vegetarian Mexican cuisine – think giant juices, and quesadillas with Chihuahua cheese, spinach, mushrooms and whole-wheat tortillas. There's also a vegan menu. (📱998-883-05-85; www.restaurantenatura.com; Blvd Kukulcán Km 9.5; breakfast M$69-109, lunch & dinner M$95-205; ⏱7:30am-10:30pm; 🛜🍴; 🚌R-1)

La Palapa Belga BELGIAN $$$

14 ✕ MAP P54, E2

One of Cancún's tastiest and most peaceful fine-dining restaurants – if you can find it. Tucked away within the Hotel Imperial Laguna's garden, this *palapa*-roofed eatery sits on a deck overlooking the lagoon. Feast on French cuisine and Belgian specialties, such as mussels in white wine broth, while taking in views of the skyline – an especially idyllic setting at sunset. (☏998-883-54-54; www.lapalapa belga.com; Quetzal 13, Hotel Imperial Laguna; mains M$235-575; ⏱3-11pm Mon-Sat; 🚍R-1)

La Destilería MEXICAN $$$

15 ✕ MAP P54, D4

This place gets the thumbs-up from locals and visitors alike. It's all good, but the chicken dishes – with goat's-cheese sauce and *mole poblano* (a sauce of chilies, spices and chocolate) – are standouts. The dining room has a huge tequila still, but if you're looking for a breeze, head out the back to the deck overlooking the lagoon. (☏998-885-10-86; www.ladestileria. com.mx; Blvd Kukulcán Km 12.65; mains M$200-400; ⏱1pm-midnight; 📶; 🚍R-1, R-2)

El Galeón del Caribe SEAFOOD $$

16 ✕ MAP P54, C7

Famed for its *pescadillas* (fried tortillas stuffed with fish), this low-key seafood *palapa* has an outdoor kitchen and lagoonside setting. It's near the southern end of the Hotel Zone and easy for in-the-know tourists to access, but its out-of-the-way location and authentic Mexican seafood make it a favorite Sunday afternoon hangout for Cancún locals too. (☏cell 998-2148175; www.facebook.com/elgaleon delcaribe; Blvd Kukulcán Km 19.4; pescadillas M$16, mains M$140-190; ⏱noon-7pm; 🚍R-1, R-2)

Drinking

The City CLUB

17 🅿 MAP P54, B3

The largest nightclub in Latin America still manages to fill up every Friday night. Frequently hosting world-famous DJs and musicians, this massive place

The City

CARL DE ABREU/ALAMY STOCK PHOTO ©

offers wild nightlife whether you're dancing on top of the central stage or watching it all from the stadium-style side levels. Due to the large crowds and 'party hearty' atmosphere, it can feel overwhelming at times. (📞998-883-33-33; www.thecitycancun.com; Blvd Kukulcán Km 9; open bar US$65; ⏰10:30pm-4am Fri; 🚌R-1)

Bar del Mar   BAR

18 📍 MAP P54, D1

One of Cancún's only beach bars open to the public. With just a few tables on the terrace and on the sand, Bar del Mar has snacks, beers and cocktails on its affordable menu. Especially good here are the tuna *tostadas* and the Bloody Caesar – a Bloody Mary prepared with habanero. There's a minimum spend of M$150. (www.facebook.com/bardelmarcancun; Blvd Kukulcán Km 6.5, Playa Tortugas; ⏰10am-6pm; 🚌R-1)

Palazzo   CLUB

19 📍 MAP P54, B3

At Palazzo, theme nights like 'Electric Party Wednesdays' and 'Red District Saturdays' give a sense of what to expect. The excitement is spread over different mezzanine levels and a massive central chandelier watches over all. (📞998-883-33-33; www.mandalatickets.com; Blvd Kukulcán Km 9; open bar US$55; ⏰11pm-4am Wed & Sat; 🚌R-1)

Coco Bongo

Mandala Beach Club   CLUB

20 🍷 MAP P54, B3

A hopping Tuesday night pool party, with all the trimmings: DJ spinning tunes, open bar and lots of bikinis. The daily daytime beach party is much more subdued. (📞998-883-33-33; www.mandalatick ets.com; Blvd Kukulcán Km 9; US$40-60; ⏰11am-6pm daily & 10:30pm-4am Tue; 🚎R-1)

Dady'O   CLUB

21 🍷 MAP P54, B3

One of Cancún's classic dance clubs. The setting is a five-level, black-walled faux cave with a two-level dance floor and what seems like zillions of laser beams and strobes. The predominant beats are Latin, house, techno and pop, and the crowd is mainly 20-something. (📞998-883-33-33; www.mandalatickets.com; Blvd Kukulcán Km 9.5; open bar US$60; ⏰10:30pm-4am Thu & Sat; 🚎R-1)

Coco Bongo   CLUB

22 🍷 MAP P54, B3

This is the spot where spring-breakers go wild, and it tends to be happening just about any day of the year. Dancing is interspersed with live acts featuring celebrity impersonators and acrobats throughout the night. (📞998-883-23-73; www. cocobongo.com; Blvd Kukulcán Km 9.5, Forum Mall; open bar US$80-195; ⏰10:30pm-5am; 🚎R-1)

Entertainment 🍷

For a wild night out hit the thumping nightclub zone between Km 9 and Km 9.5. Most of the clubs charge pricey covers but open bar is included. Exclusive **H Roof Nightclub** (Map p54, D4; 📞998-840-65-92; www.hroof.com.mx; Blvd Kukulcán Km 14.2; ⏰11pm-6am Thu-Sat; 📶) has emerged as one of the Zona Hotelera's top after-hours spots. On most nights, resident or international DJs spin lounge, hip-hop and Latino sounds. Drinks are pricey but you get a fun dance party.

Carlos'n Charlie's   BAR

23 🍷 MAP P54, B3

A cross between a restaurant and a rowdy bar, the fun-loving Carlos'n Charlie's sits in the heart of the iconic Party Center area. Get some Mexican food for lunch, grab a late-night dinner, hit the floor on Tuesday and Friday salsa nights, and maybe even dance on the bar. (📞998-265-61-80; www.carlosand charlies.com; Blvd Kukulcán Km 9; ⏰11am-2am; 🚎R-1)

Shopping

La Europea   DRINKS

24 🔒 MAP P54, D3

A gourmet liquor store with reasonable prices, knowledgeable staff and the best booze selection in town, including top-shelf tequilas and mezcals. (📞998-176-82-02; www.laeuropea.com.mx; Blvd Kulkulcán Km 12.5; 🕐10am-9pm Mon-Sat, 11am-7pm Sun; 🚍R-1)

La Isla Shopping Village MALL

25 🅐 MAP P54, D3

Unique among Cancún's malls, this is an indoor–outdoor place with canals, a 60m-high Ferris wheel, an aquarium, a movie theater, a boutique stores section and enough distractions to keep even the most inveterate hater of shopping amused. Consider picking up a bottle of *xtabentún*, a Yucatecan anise-flavored liqueur. (📞998-883-50-25; www.laislacancun.mx; Blvd Kulkulcán Km 12.5; 🕐10am-10pm; 👫; 🚍R-1)

Plaza Kukulcán MALL

26 🅐 MAP P54, D4

The largest of the indoor malls is Plaza Kukulcán. Of note here are the temporary art exhibits, the many stores selling silverwork, and La Ruta de las Indias, a shop featuring wooden models of Spanish galleons and replicas of conquistadors' weaponry and body armor. (📞998-193-01-60; www.kukulcanplaza.mx; Blvd Kulkulcán Km 13; 🕐10am-10pm; 🛜; 🚍R-1)

Escape to Isla Holbox

Holbox (hol-bosh) is defined by sandy streets, colorful Caribbean buildings, lazing dogs, and sand so fine its texture is nearly clay. The greenish waters are a unique color from the mixing of ocean currents, and on land there's a mixing too: of locals and tourists, the latter hoping to escape the hubbub of Cancún (which requires 3½ hours by bus and then a 25-minute ferry from Chiquilá).

For most people, the island is synonymous with powdery sand, but there are some lovely lagoons, low forest and more than 150 bird species, including roseate spoonbills, pelicans, herons, ibis and flamingos. Between mid-May and mid-September, massive whale sharks congregate around Isla Holbox to feed on plankton, and at night there's even the chance of seeing bioluminescent waves.

Cabañas (cabins) and bungalows are everywhere along the beach. Some of the most upscale places can be found east of town, out along the island's northern shore in what locals call the Zona Hotelera. Most budget and midrange accommodations are clustered within several blocks of the plaza. Holbox also offers a surprising number of good restaurants for such a small island, but remember that some places close early, especially during the low season.

Worth a Trip

Chichén Itzá

The most famous and best restored of the Yucatán Maya sites, Chichén Itzá is tremendously crowded but will impress even the most jaded visitor. One of the new Seven Wonders of the World, the site is unquestionably goosebump material, and the mysteries of the Maya astronomical calendar are made clear when one understands the design of the 'time temples' here.

Mouth of the Well of the Itzáes

http://chichenitza.inah.gob.mx

off Hwy 180, Pisté

adult/child under 13yr M$254/70, guided tours M$1200

8am-5pm

La Isla Shopping Village

Plaza La Fiesta   GIFTS & SOUVENIRS

27 🔒 MAP P54, B3

A location in the busy Punta Cancún area makes this big store easy to reach. Plaza La Fiesta is popular for its one-stop souvenir shopping, with most of the same products you'd find in the markets, but without the price haggling. Get colorful handicrafts, Talavera-style dishes, beachwear, jewelry and all other kinds of Cancún souvenirs in one store. (📞998-848-81-23; www. plazalafiesta.com; Blvd Kukulcán Km 9; 🕐7am-11:30pm; 🚌R-1)

Plaza Caracol   MALL

28 🔒 MAP P54, A2

An extensive array of shops and a top location in the bustling Punta Cancún area of the Hotel Zone make Plaza Caracol one of the city's most convenient shopping malls for travelers. Among other things, it offers well known brands and restaurants along with endless souvenir shops for easy vacation purchases. (📞998-883-10-38; www. caracolplaza.com; Blvd Kukulcán Km 8; 🕐10am-10pm; 🚌R-1)

Getting There

Oriente ticket offices are near the east and west sides of Pisté, and 2nd-class buses have stops throughout town. *Colectivos* (shared vans) to Valladolid (M$35, 40 minutes) enter the car park.

El Castillo

Upon entering Chichén Itzá, El Castillo (aka the Pyramid of Kukulcán; pictured) rises before you in all its grandeur. The first temple here was pre-Toltec, built around AD 800, but the present 25m-high structure, built over the old one, has the plumed serpent sculpted along the stairways and Toltec warriors represented in the doorway carvings at the top of the temple. You won't see the carvings, however, as ascending the pyramid was prohibited after a woman fell to her death in 2006.

The structure is actually a massive Maya calendar formed in stone. Each of El Castillo's nine levels is divided in two by a staircase, making 18 separate terraces that commemorate the 18 20-day months of the Maya Vague Year. The four stairways have 91 steps each; add the top platform and the total is 365, the number of days in the year. On each facade of the pyramid are 52 flat panels, which are reminders of the 52 years in the Maya calendar round.

The older pyramid inside El Castillo has a red jaguar throne with inlaid eyes and spots of jade; also lying behind the screen is a chac-mool (Maya sacrificial stone sculpture). The entrance to El Túnel, the passage up to the throne, is at the base of El Castillo's north side. You can't go in, though.

Researchers in 2015 learned that the pyramid most likely sits atop a 20m-deep cenote, which puts the structure at greater risk of collapsing.

★ **Top Tips**

o The nightly (except Mondays) attraction is the sound and light show. You must preorder your tickets online.

o Don't hesitate to haggle for a bed in Pisté in low season (May through June and August to early December).

o The heat, humidity and crowds in Chichén Itzá can be fierce, as can competition between the craft sellers who line the paths. To avoid this, try to explore the site either early in the morning or late in the afternoon.

✕ **Take a Break**

Set a block back from the highway opposite Hotel Chichén Itzá, **Restaurant Hacienda Xaybe'h d'Camara** (☏ 985-851-00-00; Calle 15A No 42; buffet lunches M$140; ⏱ 9am-5pm; 🅿 ❄ 🖉 🖐) is a large place with attractive grounds. It's popular with tours and the food is a bit overpriced, but the selection of salads makes it a good option for vegetarians.

Gran Juego de Pelota

The great ball court, the largest and most impressive in Mexico, is only one of the city's eight courts, indicative of the importance of the games held here. The court, to the left of the visitor center, is flanked by temples at either end and is bounded by towering parallel walls with stone rings cemented up high. Along the walls of the ball court are stone reliefs, including scenes of decapitations of players.

There is evidence that the ball game may have changed over the years. Some carvings show players with padding on their elbows and knees, and it is thought that they played a soccer-like game with a hard rubber ball, with the use of hands forbidden. Other carvings show players wielding bats; it appears that if a player hit the ball through one of the stone hoops, his team was declared the winner. It may be that during the Toltec period, the losing captain, and perhaps his teammates as well, was sacrificed.

The court exhibits some interesting acoustics: a conversation at one end can be heard 135m away at the other, and a clap produces multiple loud echoes.

Grupo de las Mil Columnas

This group east of El Castillo pyramid takes its name – which means 'Group of the Thousand Columns' – from the forest of pillars stretching south and east. The star attraction here is the Templo de los Guerreros (Temple of the Warriors), adorned with stucco and stone-carved ani-

Cenote Sagrado

Magic of the Equinox

At the vernal and autumnal equinoxes (around March 20 and September 22), the morning and afternoon sun produces a light-and-shadow illusion of the serpent ascending or descending the side of El Castillo's staircase. The site is mobbed on these dates, however, making it difficult to see, and after the spectacle, parts of the site are sometimes closed to the public. The illusion is almost as good in the week preceding and following each equinox (and draws much smaller crowds), and is re-created nightly (except Mondays) in the **sound and light show** (www.nochesdekukulkan.com; Tue-Sat M$483, Sun M$240) year-round. Some find the spectacle fascinating, others think it's overrated. Either way, if you're in the area around the equinox and you have your own car, it's easy to wake up early for the fiery sunrise at **Dzibilchaltún** (Place of Inscribed Flat Stones; adult M$152, parking M$20; ☉ site 8am-5pm, museum 9am-5pm Tue-Sun, cenote 9am-3:30pm) – a site north of Mérida – and then make it to Chichén Itzá by midafternoon, catching both spectacles on the same day.

mal deities. At the top of its steps is a classic reclining chac-mool figure, but ascending to it is no longer allowed.

Many of the columns in front of the temple are carved with figures of warriors. Archaeologists working in 1926 discovered a Temple of Chac-Mool lying beneath the Temple of the Warriors.

You can walk through the columns on the south side to reach the Columnata Noreste, notable for the 'big-nosed god' masks on its facade. Some have been reassembled on the ground around the statue. Just to the south are the remains of the Baño de Vapor (Steam Bath or Sweat House), with an underground oven and drains for the water. The sweat houses (there are two on site) were regularly used for ritual purification.

Cenote Sagrado

From the Platform of Skulls, a 400m rough stone *sacbé* (path) runs north (a five-minute walk) to the huge sunken well that gave this city its name. The Sacred Cenote is an awesome natural well, some 60m in diameter and 35m deep. The walls between the summit and the water's surface are ensnared in tangled vines and other vegetation.

There are ruins of a small steam bath next to the cenote.

El Caracol

Called El Caracol (The Snail) by the Spaniards for its interior spiral staircase, this observatory, to the south of the Ossuary, is one of the most fascinating and important of all Chichén Itzá's buildings (but, alas, you can't enter it). Its circular design resembles some central

Dredging Chichén's Sacred Cenote

Around the year 1900, Edward Thompson, a Harvard professor and US consul to Yucatán, bought the hacienda that included Chichén Itzá for M$750. No doubt intrigued by local stories of female virgins being sacrificed to the Maya deities by being thrown into the site's cenote, Thompson resolved to have the cenote dredged.

He imported dredging equipment and set to work. Gold and jade jewelry from all parts of Mexico and as far away as Colombia was recovered, along with other artifacts and a variety of human bones. Many of the artifacts were shipped to Harvard's Peabody Museum, but some have since been returned to Mexico.

Subsequent diving expeditions in the 1920s and 1960s turned up hundreds of other valuable artifacts. It appears that all sorts of people – children and old people, the diseased and the injured, and the young and the vigorous – were forcibly obliged to take an eternal swim in Chichén's Cenote Sagrado. (Many guides push the sacrificial angle as tourists seem fascinated by it; other experts say this aspect is way overstressed in relationship to the real objective of the site.)

The cenote is reached by walking about 400m north from the Plataforma de Venus.

highlands structures, although, surprisingly, not those of Toltec Tula.

In a fusion of architectural styles and religious imagery, there are Maya Chaac rain-god masks over four external doors facing the cardinal points. The windows in the observatory's dome are aligned with the appearance of certain stars at specific dates. From the dome the priests decreed the times for rituals, celebrations, corn planting and harvests.

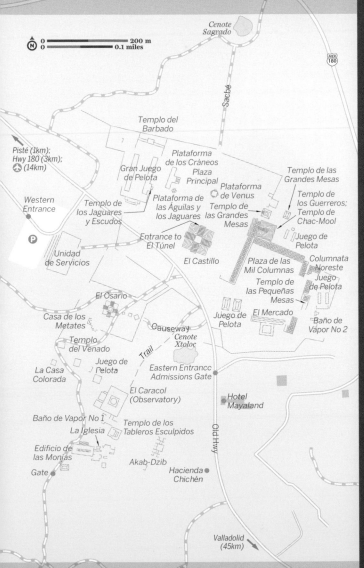

N 0   200 m
0   0.1 miles

Cenote Sagrado

MEX 180

Sacbé

Templo del Barbado

Pisté (1km);
Hwy 180 (3km);
(14km)

Plataforma de los Cráneos

Plaza Principal

Gran Juego de Pelota

Plataforma de Venus

Templo de las Grandes Mesas

Templo de los Guerreros; Templo de Chac-Mool

Western Entrance

P

Templo de los Jaguares y Escudos

Plataforma de las Águilas y los Jaguares

Templo de las Grandes Mesas

Juego de Pelota

Entrance to El Túnel

Unidad de Servicios

El Castillo

Plaza de las Mil Columnas

Columnata Noreste

Juego de Pelota

El Osario

Templo de las Pequeñas Mesas

Casa de los Metates

Causeway

El Mercado

Baño de Vápor No 2

Cenote Xtoloc

Juego de Pelota

Templo del Venado

Juego de Pelota

Trail

Eastern Entrance Admissions Gate

La Casa Colorada

El Caracol (Observatory)

Hotel Mayaland

Baño de Vapor No 1

Templo de los Tableros Esculpidos

La Iglesia

Old Hwy

Edificio de las Monjas

Akab-Dzib

Gate

Hacienda Chichén

Valladolid (45km)

Explore ✪
Isla Mujeres

Isla Mujeres has a more relaxed vibe than Cancún, and there's just enough to keep you entertained: scuba-diving and snorkeling, visiting a turtle farm or simply swimming and lazing around the island's gorgeous north shore. Sure, there are quite a few ticky-tacky tourist shops, but folks still get around by golf cart and the crushed-coral beaches are undeniably lovely.

The Short List

○ **Playa Norte (p74)** *Relaxing on the white sands and having a swim in the shallow crystalline waters.*

○ **Punta Sur (p84)** *Feeling the fresh sea breezes and marveling at the turquoise waters as you explore the island's southernmost park.*

○ **Playa Garrafón (p82)** *Seeing fish, turtles and stingrays as you snorkel the shallows off the crushed-sand beach.*

○ **Sea Hawk Divers (p82)** *Diving into the deep Caribbean blue and exploring reefs or sunken ships that seem almost otherworldly.*

○ **Isla Mujeres Turtle Farm (p76)** *Saying hello to a variety of turtles at the island's turtle farm.*

Getting There & Away

⚓ There are several points of embarkation from Cancún to reach Isla Mujeres. Most people cross on Ultramar passenger ferries. The R-1 'Puerto Juárez' city bus in Cancún serves all Zona Hotelera departure points and Puerto Juárez. If you arrive by car, daily parking fees in and around the terminals cost between M$100 and M$150, but it can be as low as M$50 if you go further from the terminal.

Isla Mujeres Map on p80

Top Sight 📷
Playa Norte

With its enticing turquoise waters and soft white sands, Playa Norte just might be the loveliest beach on the Mexican Caribbean. Sitting pretty on the island's north side, it's only about 500m long and it can definitely get crowded at times, especially during high season, but once you take a dip in the warm shallow waters you'll soon forget about that.

◎ MAP P80, D1

Picture Perfect

Frequently ranked on travel lists as one of the most beautiful beaches in the world, Playa Norte captures that idyllic postcard-perfect setting. Here the crystal-clear water rarely reaches over chest height, even as you wander further and further from shore. It also provides some of the calmest conditions imaginable for kayaking and paddleboarding. Travelers typically stick to the main stretch of beach facing toward the north-west, while locals love to relax and play in the natural pools on either side of the bridge at the northeastern side of the beach. Playa Norte sits on the northern edge of colorful downtown Isla Mujeres, right by the town's shop-lined streets and the famous Avenida Hidalgo.

Beach Clubs & Ocean-Side Dining

While nearby Cancún has hardly any beachfront restaurants outside of its resorts, Isla Mujeres is known for its many small-scale restaurants and bars with oceanfront views. Playa Norte in particular boasts a continuous row of open-air eateries and beach clubs to choose from, all offering you some of the world's most zen-inducing ocean vistas. Try the southwestern end of Playa Norte for more casual fare and a laid-back setting, like at Tuturreque 33, or visit the venues at the northeastern end, like Oceanvs, for more contemporary style. Green Demon Beach Club has become a favorite among the younger travel crowd for its health-conscious menu, flavorful cocktails, and live reggae bands on the beach every Sunday night.

★ Top Tips

o Playa Norte gets crowded during spring break in March and Mexican vacation season in July and August.

o If you're traveling with kids they'll love the shallow, calm and warm waters here.

o Playa Norte is one of the few places in the entire Mexican Caribbean where you can watch the sun set over the water. Bring your camera.

o Even if you're just on the island for a day trip, Playa Norte is an easy and enjoyable 10-minute walk from the ferry dock along the main downtown avenue.

✕ Take a Break

Buho's (p88) beach bar offers yoga classes and cold drinks under a *palapa* roof.

★ Getting There

From the town center simply walk to the northernmost point on the island.

Scientist working with a turtle bred at the hatchery

Top Sight 📷
Isla Mujeres Turtle Farm

Founded in the 1980s by a local fisherman, this sanctuary now releases as many as 100,000 hawksbill, loggerhead and green sea turtles each year. Most of the hatchlings here are liberated immediately; however, turtles needing more care are kept in pools over a longer period.

◎ MAP P80, C6

Isla Mujeres Tortugranja

📞998-888-07-05

www.facebook.com/
tortugranja.mx

Carretera Sac Bajo Km 5

M$30

🕘9am-5pm

A Working Turtle Sanctuary

Known locally by its shortened Spanish-language name, Tortugranja, the Isla Mujeres Turtle Farm works to help increase the Caribbean's at-risk sea turtle population. The thousands of sea turtle eggs laid on the beaches of Isla Mujeres every year are at great risk from humans and predators, which the staff at Tortugranja work to combat. Only one of every 1000 turtles will survive the elements but those that do make the return to the beach each year will get the same protection for their hatchlings. The farm keeps eggs in a safe area and cares for the newborn sea turtles after they hatch before releasing them into the ocean. In addition to ensuring that baby sea turtles reach their natural habitat safely, the turtle farm also keeps some groups of young sea turtles until their first year to increase their chances of survival in the wild.

Baby Turtle Release

When visiting the farm ask the staff if they will be releasing turtles later in the afternoon. It's usually done from July through November. If they are, you won't be allowed to handle the little guys but you can watch them scurry into the great big sea, which is a thrilling thing to watch if you've never seen it in person.

Turtle Nesting on Isla Mujeres

Sea turtle nesting season on Isla Mujeres runs from May through September every year. During these hot summer months, the island welcomes three different species to its shores: loggerhead, the critically endangered hawksbill (or 'carey'), and most commonly green sea turtles. Female sea turtles come up onto the shores of the island under the cover of night, dig a nest in the sand and lay their eggs. Sea turtle nests can typically contain more than 100 eggs each, and the baby sea turtles hatch within the next two months.

★ Top Tips

o Do not attempt to feed or pet the turtles.

o If you see a mother turtle laying her eggs, keep a distance of at least 30ft, stay quiet and don't shine any lights around the her (including camera flash) so that you don't frighten or disorient her.

o Beat the large crowds with an early-morning visit.

o The turtle farm posts release dates and times on its Facebook page.

o An indoor aquarium holds baby turtles, seahorses, crabs, stingrays and other fish species.

★ Getting There

A taxi from town costs M$75.

You can rent a golf cart or scooter and follow the signs heading south along the coast road.

Buggy Tour

Golf-Cart Circuit

Puttering around the island on a rented golf cart provides hours of unforgettable entertainment, so pack your swim suit and sunglasses and get ready to hit the open road. Highlights include a delicious breakfast, a turtle farm and plenty of spectacular ocean views and photo ops.

Drive Facts

Start Avenida Rueda Medina

End Town center

Length 16km; four hours

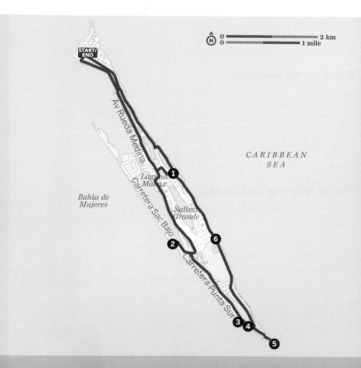

❶ Mango Café

After renting a cart in the town center, head south along **Avenida Rueda Medina** and make your first stop at Mango Café (p85) on Payo Obispo for bottomless coffee, some coconut French toast or eggs Benedict and a jaunt around the neighborhood to soak up some local flavor.

❷ Isla Mujeres Turtle Farm

Next, make your way back to Avenida Rueda Medina and follow the signs to the *tortugranja*, aka Isla Mujeres Turtle Farm (p76), where you can spend time hanging with the loggerhead, hawksbill and green turtles before they're released into the ocean. There's also a small but interesting aquarium and a pen of nurse sharks and manta rays.

❸ Hotel Garrafón de Castilla

After some quality turtle time, drive south and make a stop at one of several beach clubs along the way. The best of the lot is at Hotel Garrafón de Castilla (p82), where you can snorkel for an hour or so among colorful fish in crystalline waters.

❹ Lookout

For your next stop, continue along the same road and go just past the pricey Garrafón water park to reach a lookout point that affords a spectacular ocean view with Cancún off in the distance. It makes a fine spot to snap some pictures or simply contemplate the horizon.

❺ Punta Sur

Another photo op awaits up ahead at the oft-visited Punta Sur (p84), the southernmost point of the island. Punta Sur has a lighthouse and a weathered temple dedicated to the Maya goddess of fertility, Ixchel, but it's really the panoramic cliffside vistas that make it a worthwhile stop.

❻ East Side

After Punta Sur, the coast road loops around to the island's windswept east side, where you'll motor past several undeveloped beaches. You can stop anywhere along the way for a swim; if you do, watch out for strong currents. From this point forward it's a straight shoot back into the town center.

Orientation
The island is 8km long and 150m to 800m wide. You'll find most restaurants and hotels in the town of Isla Mujeres, with the pedestrian corridor on Hidalgo the focal point.

Isla Mujeres

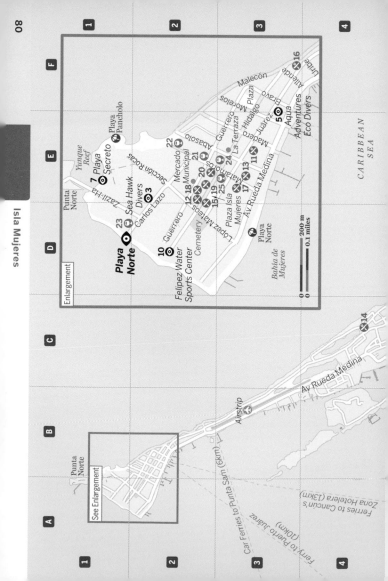

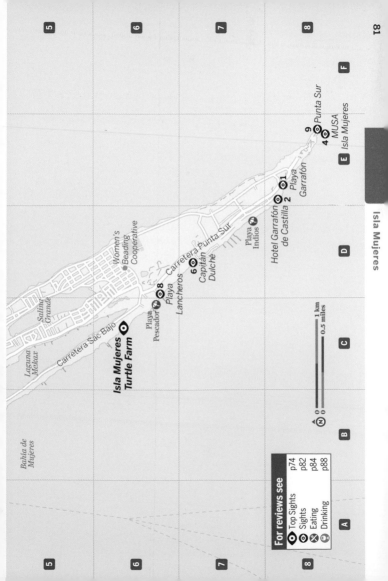

Isla Mujeres

81

Bahía de
Mujeres

Laguna
Makax

Salina
Grande

Carretera Sac Bajo

**Isla Mujeres
Turtle Farm**

Women's
Beading
Cooperative

Playa
Pescador

Playa
Lancheros

Carretera Punta Sur

Capitán Dulché

Playa
Indios

Hotel Garrafón
de Castilla

Playa
Garrafón

MUSA
Isla Mujeres

Punta Sur

For reviews see	
◉ Top Sights	p74
◉ Sights	p82
✕ Eating	p84
🍷 Drinking	p88

N

0   1 km
0   0.5 miles

Sights

Playa Garrafón BEACH

1 ⊙ MAP P80, E8

Head to this beach for excellent snorkeling. It's 6.5km from the tourist center. A cab costs M$100.

Hotel Garrafón de Castilla SNORKELING

2 ⊙ MAP P80, E8

Avoid the overpriced Playa Garrafón Reef Park and instead visit Hotel Garrafón de Castilla's beach club for a day of snorkeling in translucent waters. A taxi from town costs M$100. (🖉998-877-01-07; Carretera Punta Sur Km 6; admission M$70, snorkel-gear rental M$80; 🕙10am-6pm)

Sea Hawk Divers DIVING

3 ⊙ MAP P80, E2

Offers reef dives, intro courses, fishing trips and whale shark snorkeling tours. Sea Hawk also goes to the Isla Mujeres site of underwater sculpture museum MUSA, on the island's south side. Rents rooms, too, for US$85 to US$115. (🖉998-877-12-33; www. seahawkislamujeres.com; Carlos Lazo s/n; 1-/2-tank dives incl equipment US$80/90, intro course US$115, whale shark tour US$125; 🕙8am-6pm)

MUSA Isla Mujeres DIVING, SNORKELING

4 ⊙ MAP P80, E8

A one-of-a-kind gallery with hundreds of life-sized sculptures

Punta Sur (p84)

Island of Women?

A glimpse of the sunbathers on the beach may have you thinking that the moniker 'Island of Women' comes from the bikini-clad tourists. However, the name Isla Mujeres goes at least as far back as Spanish buccaneers, who (legend has it) kept their lovers in safe seclusion here while they plundered galleons and pillaged ports on the mainland. An alternative theory suggests that in 1517, when Francisco Hernández de Córdoba sailed from Cuba and arrived here to procure slaves, the expedition discovered a stone temple containing clay figurines of Maya goddesses; it is thought that Córdoba named the island after the icons.

Today some archaeologists believe that the island was a stopover for the Maya en route to worship their goddess of fertility, Ixchel, on Isla Cozumel. The clay idols are thought to have represented the goddess. The island may also have figured in the extensive Maya salt trade, which extended for hundreds of kilometers along the coastline.

submerged in the waters on the island's south side. At 8m deep, the Isla Mujeres Manchones gallery is ideal for first-time divers, though snorkelers are welcome as well. Organize outings through dive shops; Sea Hawk (p82) is recommended. (Museo Subacuático de Arte; ☑998-877-12-33; www.musamexico. org; Manchones reef; 1-tank dive US$70)

Aqua Adventures Eco Divers
DIVING

5 ◉ MAP P80, F3

Great option for snorkeling with whale sharks and goes to 15 sites for reef dives. (☑998-251-74-23, cell 998-3228109; www.diveislamu jeres.com; Juárez 1; 2-tank dives incl equipment from US$98, whale shark tour US$125; ⊘9am-7pm Mon-Sat, 10am-6pm Sun)

Capitán Dulché
BEACH, MUSEUM

6 ◉ MAP P80, D7

To say that this beach club has a maritime museum is a bit of a stretch, but it's as close as the island comes to having some culture, plus you get to see some cool sculptures of trenchcoated musicians playing on the water. Did we mention the bar has swings and looks like a boat? (☑cell 998-3550012; www.facebook.com/ capitandulchebeachclub; Carretera a Garrafón Km 4.5; ⊘10am-7pm; P)

Shopping

If you're headed to the island's south end, drop by the **Women's Beading Coop-erative** (Map p80, D6; cell 998-1619659; www.facebook.com/islamujeresbeadingcoop; Paseo de los Peces, Colonia La Gloria; classes M$250; 9am-5pm Mon-Sat, to 3pm Sun) and check out the colorful handmade bead jewelry made by a group of local women and children. It also offers classes if you want to learn how to make the items yourself.

Playa Secreto   BEACH

7 MAP P80, E1

The lagoon separating a large hotel complex from the rest of the island has a shallow swimming spot that's ideal for kids. Despite the depth (or lack of it), a number of pretty fish circle around the swimmers looking for handouts.

Playa Lancheros   BEACH

8 MAP P80, D6

About 5km south of town, this beach is less attractive than Playa Norte, but kayaks and stand-up paddleboards (SUPs) can be rented if you're up for some water activities. A taxi ride from town costs M$75.

Punta Sur   VIEWPOINT, GARDENS

9 MAP P80, E8

At the island's southernmost point you'll find a lighthouse, a sculpture garden and the worn remains of a temple dedicated to Ixchel, Maya goddess of the moon and fertility. Various hurricanes have pummeled the ruins over time and there's now little to see other than the sculpture garden, the sea and Cancún in the distance. Taxis from town cost M$100. (ruins M$30)

Felipez Water Sports Center   WATER SPORTS

10 MAP P80, D2

Do your acro-surf yoga on a paddleboard here. Felipez also rents kayaks and does fishing expeditions. (cell 998-5933403; nachankan@aol.com; Playa Norte, off Av Hidalgo; paddleboard or kayak per hour M$350; fishing per 4hr US$350; 8am-6pm)

Eating

Javi's Cantina   SEAFOOD $$$

11 MAP P80, E3

More like a restaurant than a cantina, but Javi's does have happy hour and live music. The menu consists of seafood, choice beef cuts, chicken and various salad and veggie options. A house specialty is the fresh-caught, parmesan-crusted fish fillet with tamarind sauce. Dine in the front room or sit back in the rear courtyard with a pleasant terrace. Online reservations only. (www.javiscantina.com; Juárez 12; mains M$225-550; ☺5-10:30pm; 📶📷)

Lola Valentina FUSION $$$

12 🍴 MAP P80, E2

Overlooking the quieter north side of the restaurant strip, Lola does excellent Mexican fusion with dishes such as coconut shrimp with a mango-Sriracha-soy dipping sauce. Also on the menu are several vegan, gluten-free items, and the decidedly non-vegan, non-GF Latin Surf 'n' Turf. It's added swings at the bar (fun!) and redone its tasty cocktail menu (yum!). Cash only. (📞998-315-94-79; www.facebook.com/lolavalentinaislamujeres; Hidalgo s/n; mains M$145-410; ☺8am-11pm; 📶📷)

Bobo's FISH & CHIPS $$

13 🍴 MAP P80, E3

This bar and grill fries up excellent locally caught triggerfish for its popular fish and chips and there's malt vinegar to go along with it (a rare find in Mexico). Bobo's is also known for its burgers and convivial streetside bar. (www.facebook.com/bobosfishchips; Matamoros 14; mains M$95-115; ☺3-11pm)

Mango Café BREAKFAST $$

14 🍴 MAP P80, C4

See the south side of town and drop by Mango Café for some

Tikin Xic (chicken, guacamole, salsa and rice)

self-serve coffee and a hearty Caribbean-inspired breakfast. The hot items here are coconut French toast and eggs Benedict in a curry hollandaise sauce. It's a short bike or cab ride away, about 3km south of the ferry terminal. (☎998-400-19-04; www.facebook.com/mangocafeisla; Payo Obispo 101, Colonia Meterológico; mains M$100-170; ⏲7am-3pm Tue & Wed, to 9pm Thu-Mon; 🖥)

Rooster CAFE $$

 15 MAP P80, E2

The undeniable king of the breakfast providers on the island is this cute little cafe with tables out front and chilly air-con inside. The menu covers the classics and throws in a couple of inventive twists, such as eggs Benedict with lobster, and all is served up with excellent coffee and attentive service. (☎998-274-01-52; www.facebook.com/roosterislamujeres; Hidalgo 26; breakfasts M$107-225; ⏲7am-11pm; 🖥)

La Lomita MEXICAN $$

16 MAP P80, F3

The 'Little Hill' serves good, cheap Mexican food in a small, colorful setting. Seafood and chicken dishes predominate. Try the fantastic bean and avocado soup, or the ceviche (seafood marinated in lemon or lime juice, garlic and seasonings). The walls are cutely painted and outdoors there's a little alfresco dining section with umbrellas. (☎cell 998-1799431; www.facebook.com/restaurantlalomita;

Fishermen in Isla Mujeres

Juárez Sur 25; mains M$120-200;
⊙9am-10pm)

Olivia
MEDITERRANEAN $$$

17 ✖ MAP P80, E3

This delightful Israeli-run res-
taurant makes everything from
scratch, from Moroccan-style fish
served on a bed of couscous to
chicken shawarmas wrapped in
fresh-baked pita bread. Ask for a
candlelit table out back in the gar-
den, and save room for the house-
made cherry ice cream. Usually
closes September to mid-October.
Reservations recommended.
(☎998-877-17-65; www.olivia-isla
-mujeres.com; Matamoros s/n; mains
M$155-280; ⊙5-9:45pm Mon-Sat; 🤝)

Ruben's Restaurant
MEXICAN $

18 ✖ MAP P80, E2

There's nothing fancy about
this little diner, but homemade
Mexican food and great service
are guaranteed. Regulars usually
go for the daily set menu, which
includes soup, salad and a main
dish. There are also a few gringo-
friendly items on the menu, for
example the 'super burrito.' Aguas
(fruit juices) are always refreshing.
(rubenchavez_77@hotmail.com; Guer-
rero 18; mains M$50-145, set menu
M$95; ⊙8am-9pm Mon-Sat; 🤝)

Qubano
CUBAN $$

19 ✖ MAP P80, E2

Here you get a different sound
than the neighboring restaurants –
Cuban son music selections as

Seafood & Eating Out
🍽

Seafood can't get fresher
than here, so plan on eating
as much as possible. The
restaurants are a mixed bag
and sometimes pricier than
comparable mainland food. A
supermarket on the plaza has
a solid selection of groceries,
baked goods and snacks.

For cheap eats, check the
Mercado Municipal (Map
p80, E2; Guerrero s/n, btwn López
Mateos & Matamoros; mains
M$50-120; ⊙7am-4pm) during
the day and the food stalls on
the plaza outside the Iglesia
de la Inmaculada Concepción
at night.

opposed to bad disco remixes.
Apart from that, you get a change
from Mexican fare with ropa vieja
(slow-cooked shredded beef),
Cuban sandwiches and mojitos.
(☎998-877-12-73; www.facebook.com/
qubanoIsla; Hidalgo s/n; mains M$130-
205; ⊙noon-10:30pm Mon-Fri, from
5pm Sat; 🤝)

Aluxes Coffee Shop
CAFE $$

20 ✖ MAP P80, E2

Aluxes serves bagels, baguettes
and mighty fine banana bread,
and it's one of the friendliest joints
in town. (www.aluxesisla.com; Mata-
moros 11; breakfast M$60-85, lunch
& dinner M$95-350; ⊙8am-10pm
Wed-Mon; 🤝)

Drinking

La Tablita
BAR

21 🚇 MAP P80, E2

For a little local flavor, spend a lazy afternoon over cold drinks and free snacks in this atmospheric, fan-cooled Caribbean house. The jukebox selection of Spanish-language tracks is *muy buena*. (Av Guerrero s/n; ⏱noon-8pm Mon-Sat)

Poc-Na Hostel
BAR

22 🚇 MAP P80, E2

Has a lobby bar with nightly live music and a beachfront bar with thumping music and more hippies than all the magic buses in the world. It's a scene, and an entertaining one at that. Drinks aren't expensive, but aren't magically good either. (☎998-877-00-90; www.pocna.com; Matamoros 26; ⏱7pm-3am; 🛜)

Buho's
BAR

23 🚇 MAP P80, D1

The quintessential swinger experience. Literally: it has swings at the bar. You can also take morning and afternoon yoga classes here. Any closer to the beach and you'd be in the water. (☎998-877-03-01; Carlos Lazo 1, Playa Norte; ⏱9am-11pm; 🛜)

El Patio
BAR

24 🚇 MAP P80, E3

The self-proclaimed 'house of music' has an open-air patio and

Isla Mujeres sign, El Malecón

BYELIKOVA OKSANA/SHUTTERSTOCK ©

Salsa Dancing

Drinks and food are nothing special at **La Terraza** (Map p80, E3; 2nd fl, Hidalgo s/n, cnr Abasolo; ⏰4pm-midnight), but if the Cuban salsa band is playing it's definitely worth sticking around for some dancing.

rooftop terrace where you can catch mediocre rock cover bands and relatively subdued acoustic sets. Happy hour is from 5pm to 7pm, with food specials as well as discount drinks. (www.facebook.com/elpatioislamujeres; Hidalgo 17; ⏰3:30pm-midnight; 🛜)

Fayne's   BAR

25 🔕 MAP P80, E3

This disco-bar and grill often features live reggae, salsa and other Caribbean sounds. (www.facebook.com/faynesbar; Hidalgo 12; ⏰11am-2am)

Explore ✦

Playa del Carmen

Playa del Carmen ranks right up there with Tulum as one of the Riviera's trendiest spots. Sitting coolly on the lee side of Cozumel, the town's beaches are jammed with super-fit Europeans. The waters aren't as clear as those of Cancún or Cozumel, and the sand isn't quite as powder-perfect as it is further north, but still Playa grows in popularity.

The Short List

○ **Diving (p98)** *Taking the plunge into underwater cave systems and diving with bull sharks around ocean reefs.*

○ **Fusion (p105)** *Hanging at a beach bar with live tunes and fire dancers and then taking a bar crawl to keep the party rolling.*

○ **Río Secreto (p98)** *Wading deep into a 1km-long underground cavern full of gorgeous stalagmites and stalactites.*

○ **Quinta Avenida (p99)** *Wining, dining and shopping for arts and crafts along downtown Playa's pedestrian thoroughfare.*

Getting There & Away

🚢 Passenger ferries depart frequently to Cozumel from Calle 1 Sur, where you'll find two companies with ticket booths, and a terminal south of Playa operates car ferries to Cozumel.

🚌 Playa has two bus terminals; each sells tickets and provides information for at least some of the other's departures.

🚐 *Colectivos* are a great option for cheap travel southward to Tulum and north to Cancún.

Playa del Carmen Map on p96

Parque Dos Ojos

Top Sights 📷
Riviera Maya's Cenotes

Playa del Carmen makes a good base to explore the Riviera Maya's many cenotes, most of which are set in gorgeous jungles. Water activities at cenotes include swimming, snorkeling and diving in caves or caverns. Cave diving, which can be very dangerous, is for certified divers only and must be arranged through a dive shop.

One look and it's easy to see why the Maya thought cenotes (limestone sinkholes) were sacred: fathomless cerulean pools, dancing shafts of light, darkened chambers. Even if you don't buy the spiritual aspects, they're still awe-inspiring examples of nature's beauty – and there are thousands of them dotting the peninsula.

Parque Dos Ojos

About 1km south of amusement park Xel-Há is the turnoff to the enormous **Dos Ojos cave system** (☎cell 984-1600906; www.parquedosojos. com; Hwy 307 Km 124; 1-/2-tank dive M$1850/2600, snorkeling M$470; ⏱8am-5pm). Operating as a sustainable-tourism project by the local Maya community, Dos Ojos offers guided snorkeling tours of some amazing underwater caverns, where you float past illuminated stalactites and stalagmites in an eerie wonderland. For diving, you must go with a dive shop.

Cristalino Cenote

On the west side of the highway, 23km south of Playa del Carmen, **Cristalino** (☎cell 984-8043941; Hwy 307 Km 269; adult/child 3-12yr M$150/100, diving M$200; ⏱8am-6pm) is one of a series of wonderful cenotes. It's easily accessible, only about 70m from the entrance gate to the Barceló Maya Beach Resort, which is just off the highway. Great for diving (or just launching yourself off the rocks into the water below).

Cenote Azul

Conveniently located right off the main highway, **Cenote Azul** (www.facebook.com/ CenoteAzulRM; Hwy 307, Km 266; adult/child 4-8yr M$100/60; ⏱8:30am-5:30pm) is one of the easi-st Riviera Maya cenotes to visit. It's also one the region's most spectacularly beautiful ⁜ural attractions. Leap off the small cliff into clear waters at the deep end of the cenote, pend the afternoon snorkeling among the on the shallow side. Cash only.

★ Top Tips

● At some cenotes you can rent gear, but, when in doubt, take your own.

● Note that cenotes close to large cities are often polluted.

✕ Take a Break

In striking distance of the best cenotes near Playa del Carmen, **Chamicos** (☎cell 984-1150260; mains M$160-350; ⏱11am-5pm; P) does fresh-caught fish and seafood in simple preparations right on the beach. You may not have white linen and fine china, but you can't ask for a nicer view, and the plastic chairs and tables are nicely shaded by palm trees.

Walking Tour 🥾

Bar Crawl

In Playa del Carmen, you'll find everything from mellow, tranced-out lounge bars to thumping beachfront discos, and why not try them all? Whether it's martinis, salsa or even fire dancing that lights you up, this raucous beach town has you covered. The party generally starts on Quinta Avenida then heads down toward the beach on Calle 12.

Walk Facts

Start Fusion

End Corner of 1 Avenida Norte and Calle 12 Norte

Length 2.5km; 5½ hours

❶ Fusion

Get things rolling at beach bar Fusion (p105) at around 10.30pm. Grab one of the candlelit tables on the sand and chat over drinks and live music. Stick around for at least an hour so as not to miss a cool fire-dance show on the beach.

❷ Dirty Martini Lounge

After watching the fire dancers doing their thing, head up Calle 6 Norte, then turn right at Calle 10 Norte and then walk north to the next stop, Dirty Martini Lounge (p103). Order a round of martinis (shaken, not stirred) and chill out in one of Playa's coolest bars, where you can grab the karaoke mike if you're feeling inspired by some liquid courage.

❸ La Verbena

Next, after quite possibly embarrassing yourself, go left on Calle 12 Norte and then hang a right on pedestrian thoroughfare Quinta Avenida (5 Av). It's about a 1km stroll north along the Avenida to reach Calle 34 Norte, where you're going to turn left and walk a half-block to La Verbena (p105), one of Playa's classic live music bars with bands often playing hip-shaking

cumbias (music originating from Colombia) and ska. At this hour, you probably won't find a table and it can get pretty steamy in the back room where the groups play, but a cold beer usually helps.

❹ La Bodeguita del Medio

Once you've had your fill of live tunes in the self-proclaimed 'House of Fine Music,' make your way over to La Bodeguita del Medio (p103) for some late-night salsa grooves. It's just a stumble or two away from La Verbena, 60m north along Quinta Avenida. Get into the Cuban spirit with a round of mojitos, then step onto the dance floor and show off those salsa moves that you've been practicing.

❺ Dirty Martini Otra Vez?

After lights out at the Bodeguita, make your way back toward the starting point of the bar crawl. At this juncture you can return to Dirty Martini Lounge for a nightcap, or you can hit the nearby corner of 1 Avenida Norte and Calle 12 Norte, where you'll find an after-hours street party and thumping nightclubs competing for decibel levels. Or simply call it a night.

Playa del Carmen

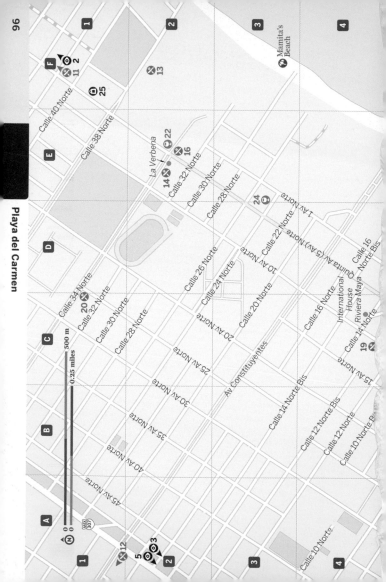

Mamita's Beach

La Verbena

500 m
0.25 miles

Calle 40 Norte
Calle 38 Norte
Calle 34 Norte
Calle 32 Norte
Calle 30 Norte
Calle 28 Norte
Calle 26 Norte
Calle 24 Norte
Calle 22 Norte
Calle 20 Norte
Calle 16 Norte
Calle 14 Norte
Calle 12 Norte Bis
Calle 12 Norte
Calle 10 Norte Bis
Calle 10 Norte

Calle 32 Norte
Calle 30 Norte
Calle 28 Norte

Calle 24 Norte
Calle 22 Norte (5 AV) Norte
Calle 20 Norte
Calle 16 Norte Bis
Calle 16 Norte
Calle 14 Norte

20 AV Norte
25 AV Norte
30 AV Norte
35 AV Norte
40 AV Norte
45 AV Norte

10 AV Norte
1 AV Norte
15 AV Norte

Quinta AV (5 AV) Norte
Av Constituyentes
International House
Riviera Maya

MEX
307

Phocea Mexico

DIVING

1 🎯 MAP P96, C6

French, English and Spanish are spoken at Phocea Mexico. The shop does dives with bull sharks (US$90) for advanced divers, usually from November to March. (📞 984-873-12-10; www.phocea-mexico. com; Calle 10 Norte s/n; 2 tank dive incl gear US$104, cenote dives incl gear US$150; ⏱ 7:30am-8pm)

Punta Esmeralda

BEACH

2 🎯 MAP P96, F1

Emerald Point has become a favorite beach among Playa del Carmen locals, set on the northern edge of the city. Here, a shallow cenote provides a calm coastal pool where kids love to play, and the soft white sand beach is an idyllic spot to spread your beach towel for a day by the ocean. (via 5 Av Norte, just north of Calle 112 Norte; admission free; P)

Río Secreto

ADVENTURE

3 🎯 MAP P96, A2

Hike and swim through a 1km-long underground cavern 5km south of Playa del Carmen. Some aspects are hyped, but there is a lot that is just plain awesome. (📞 998-113-19-05; www.riosecreto.com; Carretera 307 Km 283.5; adult/child 4-12yr from US$79/40; ⏱ tours 8am-2pm)

Aquarium

AQUARIUM

4 🎯 MAP P96, C5

An impressive three-story aquarium with 200 marine species and 45 exhibits. One of the few options in Playa for non-beach days. (El Acuario de Playa; 📞 998-287-53-13, 984-879-44-62; www.elacuariodeplaya. com; 2nd fl, Plaza Calle Corazon, Calle 14 Norte 148, ; M$270; ⏱ 11am-10pm)

Flora, Fauna y Cultura de México

VOLUNTEERING

5 🎯 MAP P96, A2

Contact this Xcaret-based organization to assist with conservation efforts at Playa Xcacel as turtles come ashore to lay their eggs. You can arrange a minimum one-month stay (M$2000) from May to October, which includes three daily meals and rustic lodging in a *palapa,* but you'll need to bring your own hammock. Volunteering for adults only. (📞 984-871-52-89, cell 984-1880626; www.florafaunay cultura.org; Hwy 307 Km 282, v park office; ⏱ 9am-5pm Mon-Fri)

Parque la Ceiba

PARK

6 🎯 MAP P96, A7

Two blocks west of the highway, this pretty park has play areas for kids, shady picnic spots and walking trails as well as activities such as movie screenings, yoga classes and the occasional concert. Every third Saturday of the month, La

Ceiba hosts a crafts market with Maya artisans selling their wares. (📞984-859-23-27; www.facebook.com/parquelaceiba; 1 Av Sur, cnr Diagonal 60 Sur, Colonia Ejidal; admission free; ⏰7am-8:30pm Tue-Sat, 8am-5pm Sun)

Quinta Avenida

STREET

7 👁 MAP P96, C5

Restaurants, bars, stores and crafts stalls line a 2km stretch of this busy pedestrian thoroughfare.

Parque Fundadores

SQUARE

8 👁 MAP P96, B7

Playa del Carmen's most iconic park is bordered by the famous Quinta Avenida on one side and by a popular local beach on the other side. Here, kids can run around on the playground or try some Mexican treats at the row of fruit stands. In the afternoons, small crowds gather under the Portal Maya statue to enjoy the sunset. (cnr 5 Av Sur & Av Juárez)

Fisherman's Cooperative

FISHING/SNORKELLING

9 👁 MAP P96, E5

Support the locals and head to the fisherman's cooperative at this beachfront kiosk. It does four-hour fishing or snorkeling trips, or you can combine both activities. Refreshments are included. (📞cell 984-1276230, cell 984-8795161; coopturmarcaribe@hotmail.com; Calle 16 Bis s/n; up to 4 people US$220, per extra person US$10; ⏰6am-8pm)

Playa del Carmen Sights

Quinta Avenida

ANJUCHKA/GETTY IMAGES ©

Museo Frida Kahlo Riviera Maya

MUSEUM

10 ⊙ MAP P96, C6

This 'museum' is mainly info *about* Kahlo rather than displays of her artwork. It's also small. But if you're looking for something to do on a non-beach day, you could come here and learn about one of Mexico's most famous icons. (☏984-980-05-95; www.museofridakahlo rivieramaya.org; 5 Av Norte s/n, cnr Calle 8; US$15; ⏱9am-11pm; P)

Eating

Passion

BASQUE $$$

11 🍴 MAP P96, F1

With a French-Basque-inspired menu created by 8-Michelin-starred chef Martin Berasategui,

MALGOSIA S/SHUTTERSTOCK ©

this is unquestionably one of Playa's finest restaurants. Diners can order from the à la carte menu or opt for the exquisite seven-course tasting menu. Reserve ahead and dress appropriately for a meal served in an elegant dining room at the Paradisus Hotel. (☏984-877-39-00; www.passion bymb.com; 5 Av Norte, Paradisus Hotel; mains M$600-1100, tasting menu M$1950; ⏱6-9:30pm Mon-Sat; P ❄ 📶)

Ferron's Jerk Chicken

JAMAICAN $$

12 🍴 MAP P96, A1

Venture out to the seldom-visited side of Playa for some fine Jamaican jerk chicken and a cool reggae vibe. Combo meals include sweet-and-spicy grilled chicken, corn on the cob, coleslaw and a dinner roll. There's also grilled spicy pork ribs. (☏984-206-19-41; www.facebook.com/ferronsjerkchicken; Av 105 Norte 3, cnr Av Constituyentes; mains M$89-169; ⏱noon-6pm Tue-Sun; 📶)

La Cueva del Chango

MEXICAN $$

13 🍴 MAP P96, F2

The 'Monkey's Cave,' known for its fresh and natural ingredients, has seating in a jungly *palapa* setting or a verdant garden out back. Service is friendly, but the kitchen can be slow. The food is delicious; try the stuffed ancho chili peppers and *chilaquiles* (fried tortillas bathed in sauce). (☏984-147-0 www.lacuevadelchango.com; C Norte s/n, btwn 5 Av Norte &

breakfast M$90-114, lunch & dinner
M$168-198; ⏰8am-10:30pm, to 2pm
Sun; 📶)

Axiote
MEXICAN $$$

14 🍴 MAP P96, E2

Putting a gourmet twist on tacos, *tostadas* and Mexican regional dishes, Axiote's diverse menu features creative treats like fish tacos with a sausage-avocado sauce and bone marrow topped with a refried bean and chili *guajillo* salsa. The casual *palapa* restaurant can get packed on weekends but there are some cool bars nearby if you need to kill some time. (📞984-803-17-27; www.axiote.rest; Calle 34 Norte; mains M$230-268; ⏰1:30-11pm)

La Famiglia
ITALIAN $$$

15 🍴 MAP P96, C5

Pay a visit to the family and enjoy superb wood-fired pizza and handmade pasta, ravioli and gnocchi. Playa is a magnet for Italian restaurants, but this definitely ranks among the best of them. (📞984-803-53-50; www.facebook.com/lafamigliapdc; 10 Av Norte s/n, cnr Calle 10 Norte; mains M$130-390; ⏰noon-11pm Tue-Sat, from 3pm Sun; 📶)

Chez Céline
BREAKFAST $

16 🍴 MAP P96, E2

...ood, healthy breakfasts and a ...ge of yummy baked goods ...hat keeps this French-run ...-cafe busy. (📞984-803-34-

Spanish Lessons 📓

Playa has a couple of good language schools and you'll find plenty of people to practice Spanish with, especially if you venture out beyond the tourist center. **International House Riviera Maya** (Map p96, C4; 📞984-803-33-88; www.ihrivieramaya.com; Calle 14 Norte 141; per week US$230) offers 20 hours of Spanish classes per week. You can stay in residence-hall rooms (US$36), even if you're not taking classes, but the best way to learn the language is to take advantage of the school's homestays (including breakfast, US$33 to US$39) with Mexican host families.

80; www.chezceline.com.mx; cnr 5 Av Norte & Calle 34 Norte; breakfast M$72-129; ⏰7:30am-11pm; ❄📶)

Asere Ke Bola
CUBAN $

17 🍴 MAP P96, A6

If you're pinching pesos, hit this mornings-only, Cuban-owned corner spot and try the tasty *torta de lechón,* a crunchy roast-pork sandwich sprinkled with consommé and topped with pickled red onion; it's very hard to eat just one! Located in the Banorte parking lot. (cnr Hwy 307 & Av Juárez; tacos & tortas M$13-25; ⏰7am-1pm)

Beaches of Playa del Carmen

Avid beachgoers won't be disappointed here. Playa's lovely white-sand beaches are much more accessible than Cancún's: just head down to the ocean, stretch out and enjoy. Numerous restaurants front the beach in the tourist zone and many hotels in the area offer an array of water-sport activities.

If crowds aren't your thing, go north of Calle 38, where a few scrawny palms serve for shade. Here the beach extends for uncrowded kilometers, making for good camping, but you need to be extra careful with your belongings, as thefts are a possibility.

Some women go topless in Playa (though it's not common in most of Mexico, and is generally frowned upon by locals). **Mamita's Beach**, north of Calle 28, is considered the best place to let loose and it's LGBTIQ-friendly to boot.

About 3km south of the ferry terminal, past a group of all-inclusives, you'll find a refreshingly quiet stretch of beach that sees relatively few visitors.

Kaxapa Factory
SOUTH AMERICAN $

18   MAP P96, B5

The specialty at this Venezuelan restaurant on the park are *arepas* (delicious corn flatbread stuffed with your choice of shredded beef, chicken or beans and plantains). There are many vegetarian and gluten-free options here and the refreshing, fresh-made juices go nicely with just about everything on the menu. (984-803-50-23; www.kaxapa-factory.com; Calle 10 Norte s/n; mains M$65-145; 8am-10pm Tue-Sun;)

Don Sirloin
MEXICAN $

19   MAP P96, C4

Al pastor (marinated pork) and sirloin beef are sliced right off the spit at this popular late-night taco joint, which now has four locations in Playa. (984-148-04-24; www.donsirloin.com; 10 Av Norte s/n; tacos M$14-65; 2pm-6am;)

Los Aguachiles
SEAFOOD $$

20   MAP P96, C1

Done up in Mexican cantina style yet with one big difference: the menu – consisting of tacos, *tostadas* and the like – was designed by a chef. The artfully prepared tuna *tostadas* found here won't be in any of the neighborhood watering holes. (984-859-14-42; www.facebook.com/losaguachilesrm; Cal 34 Norte s/n; tostadas M$39-85, M$135-340; 12:30-9pm;)

Drinking

Dirty Martini Lounge
BAR

21  MAP P96, C5

The Dirty Martini Lounge doesn't have a foam machine, there's no mechanical bull and there's minimal nudity – a refreshing change for crazy Playa. The decor is something you'd find in the American West, with comfy cowhide upholstery and brown wood panels, and it's a place where you can sip something tasty while actually hearing yourself think. (www.facebook.com/dirtymartinilounge; 1 Av Norte 234; ⏰noon-2am, to 3am Fri & Sat)

La Bodeguita del Medio
DANCING

22 MAP P96, E2

The writing is literally on the walls (and on the lampshades, and pretty much everywhere) at this Cuban restaurant-bar. After a few mojitos you'll be dancing the night away to live *cubana* music. Get here at 7pm from Tuesday to Friday for free salsa lessons. (☎984-803-39-50; www.labodeguitadelmedio.com.mx; 5 Av Norte s/n, cnr Calle 34 Norte; ⏰12:30pm-2am; 🛜)

Playa 69
GAY

23 MAP P96, B6

This popular gay dance club proudly features foreign strippers

Los Aguachiles

AL ARGUETA/ALAMY STOCK PHOTO ©

from such far-flung places as Australia and Brazil, and it stages weekend drag-queen shows. It may also open Tuesdays at key vacation times. Find it at the end of the narrow alley. (www.facebook.com/sesentaynueveplaya; off 5 Av Norte, btwn Calles 4 & 6; cover after 10pm M$60; ⏰9pm-4am Wed-Sun)

Caiman Tugurio   BAR

24 🍺 MAP P96, E3

Kind of hard to find in Playa – a bar with cool music where you can just go for a few relaxed drinks. No cover, no dance floor, just a great place to chill with friends. (📞984-147-16-95; www.facebook.com/caimantugurio24; Calle 24 Norte; ⏰9pm-2am)

Shopping

Tierra Huichol   ARTS & CRAFTS

25 🔒 MAP P96, F1

Tierra Huichol's Playa del Carmen store sells intricate yarn art and colorful beaded animal figurines crafted by indigenous Huichol artists from the Pacific coast states of Jalisco and Nayarit. International delivery service available. (📞984-803-59-54; www.tierrahuichol.com; 5 Av Norte s/n, btwn Calles 38 & 40; ⏰10am-11pm)

Artemanos   ARTS & CRAFTS

26 🔒 MAP P96, B7

A small store along the Quinta Avenida where you can pick up

Quinta Avenida (p99)

PLAYA DEL CARMEN/SHUTTERSTOCK ©

Best for Live Music

Fusion (Map p96, C6; ☎ cell 984-879174; www.facebook.com/fusion beachbarcuisine; Calle 6 Norte s/n; ☺ 8am-1am) This beachside bar and grill stages live music, along with a fun belly-dancing and fire-dancing show. The fire dancing comes later in the evening (around 11pm). From 6pm and on, it's just a cool spot to have a beer or cocktail and listen to rock, reggae and Latin sounds.

La Verbena (Map p96, E2; ☎ cell 984-1289991; www.facebook.com/laverbenaplaya; Calle 34 Norte s/n; ☺ 6pm-2am) The self-proclaimed 'House of Fine Music House' hosts a wide range of live music, from hip-shaking cumbias (music originating from Colombia) to reggae and ska beats. On warm nights, it can get downright steamy in the back room where the bands play, but you'll forget about it after swigging down some cold beers.

alebrijes (colorful wooden animal figures) from Oaxaca, silver jewelry and bead and yarn art crafted by indigenous Huicholes. (☎984-803-12-72; www.facebook.com/artemanosartemexicano; 5 Av Norte; ☺ 9am-11pm)

Paseo del Carmen

27 🗺 MAP P96, A7   MALL

A Mediterranean-style open-air plaza with stores selling mostly foreign brands, and several cafes and small eateries in the passage-ways. (☎984-803-37-89; www.paseodelcarmen.com; 10 Av Sur 8; ☺ 11am-10pm)

Worth a Trip 👀
Laguna Bacalar

Laguna Bacalar, the peninsula's largest lagoon, comes as a surprise in this region of scrubby jungle. More than 60km long with a bottom of sparkling white sand, this crystal-clear lagoon offers opportunities for camping, swimming, kayaking and simply lazing around, amid a color palette of blues, greens and shimmering whites. Some would say this area is the 'new' Tulum.

Getting There & Away

Buses don't enter town, but taxis and some colectivos will drop you at the town square. Buses arrive at Bacalar's **ADO station** (☏983-833-31-63; www.ado.com.mx; Hwy 307 s/n, btwn Calles 28 & 30). From there it's about a 10-block walk southeast to the main square, or you can grab a local taxi for M$20.

If you're driving from the north and want to reach the town and fort, take the first Bacalar exit and continue several blocks before turning left (east) down the hill. From Chetumal, head west to catch Hwy 307 north; after 25km on the highway you'll reach the signed right turn for (p93) and Avenida Costera, also known as Avenida 1.

Fortress

The fortress above the lagoon was built in 1733 to protect Spanish colonists from pirate attacks and rebellions by local indigenous people. It also served as an important outpost for the Spanish in the War of the Castes. In 1859 it was seized by Maya rebels, who held the fort until Quintana Roo was conquered by Mexican troops in 1901.

Today, with formidable cannons still on its ramparts, the fortress remains an imposing sight. It houses a museum that exhibits colonial armaments and uniforms from the 17th and 18th centuries.

Balneario

This beautiful public swimming spot (Av Costera s/n; cnr Calle 14; ☉9am–6pm) lies several blocks south of the fort, along Avenida Costera. Admission is free, but parking costs M$10.

★ Top Tips

○ While many places still cater to the budget or midrange traveler, there's a growing number of high-end options cropping up in town and along the lagoon's shores.

○ Around the town plaza, you'll find ATMs, a money exchange office, a small grocery store, a taxi stand and tourist information office.

○ Most places in Bacalar are within walking distance.

✗ Take a Break

The slooow-food experience at **Nixtamal** (☏cell 983-1347651; www.facebook.com/nixtamalcocinaafuegoyceniza; López Mateos 525, cnr Calle 12; mains M$120–280, lobster M$1500; ☉7–11pm Wed–Mon; 🔊) pushes your patience to the limit, but grill master Rodrigo Estrada makes it well worth the wait. The candlelit, open-air restaurant stages live music on weekends.

Explore
Tulum

Tulum's spectacular coastline – with all its confectioner-sugar sands, cobalt water and balmy breezes – makes it one of the top beaches in Mexico. Where else can you get all that and a dramatically situated Maya ruin? There's also excellent cave and cavern diving, fun cenotes and a variety of lodgings and restaurants to fit every budget.

The Short List

○ **Tulum Ruins (p110)** *Marveling at cliffside Maya ruins and cooling off with a refreshing swim in the ocean below.*

○ **Gran Cenote (p115)** *Taking the plunge into a limestone sinkhole and snorkeling or diving in caverns.*

○ **IK Lab (p113)** *Wandering barefoot through one of the most surreal art galleries you'll ever see and experiencing its unique interactive vibe.*

○ **Uyo Ochel Maya (p113)** *Swimming in an ancient Maya canal and nature-watching on a boat tour through a lagoon ecosystem.*

○ **Salsa Sunday (p115)** *Taking free salsa classes and dancing to live music at a beach bar.*

Getting There & Away

🚌 The **ADO bus terminal** (Map p112, C6; 📞984-871-21-22; www.ado.com.mx; Av Tulum, btwn Calles Alfa Norte & Jupiter Norte; ⊗24hr) is simple but adequate, with some chairs for waiting, but not much else.

🚌 *Colectivos* leave from Avenida Tulum for Playa del Carmen (p112, C6; M$45, 45 minutes). Colectivos to Cobá (Map p112, C6; Osiris Norte s/n, cnr Av Tulum; M$70) depart every two hours or so from 9am to 6pm.

Tulum Map on p112

Top Sight 📷
Tulum Ruins

Sitting pretty on a bluff high above gleaming tur-quoise waters, these Maya ruins may not have the imposing structures of, say, Chichén Itzá, but no other archaeological site in Mexico comes close to offering stunning vistas like this.

◉ MAP P112, C2

www.inah.gob.mx

Hwy 307 Km 230

admission M$70, parking M$180, tours from M$5

🕐 8am-5pm

El Castillo

This watchtower was appropriately named El Castillo (The Castle) by the Spaniards. Note the Descending God in the middle of its facade, and the Toltec-style 'Kukulcánes' (plumed serpents) at the corners, echoing those at Chichén Itzá.

Templo de las Pinturas

This temple's decoration was among the most elaborate at Tulum and included relief masks and colored murals on an inner wall. The murals have been partially restored, but are nearly impossible to make out.

Estructura 25

Structure 25 has some interesting columns on its raised platform and, above the main doorway (on the south side), a beautiful stucco frieze of the Descending God.

Templo del Dios Descendente

This temple gets its name from a relief figure of a Descending God depicted above the building's door. The Descending God has become known as perhaps the most iconic image of Tulum.

Casa del Cenote

This house was named for the small sinkhole at its southern base, where you can sometimes see the glitter of little silvery fish as they turn sideways in the murky water.

Templo de la Estela

The restored Templo de la Estela (Temple of the ...ela) is also known as the Temple of the Initial ...es. Stela 1, now in the British Museum, was ...d here.

★ **Top Tips**

○ To beat the crowds get to the site between 8am and 9am (it's also cooler then).

○ You'll find cheaper parking east of the main lot.

✗ **Take a Break**

Before hitting the ruins swing by Taquería Honorio (p116) and get some early morning tacos.

★ **Getting There**

Northbound Playa del Carmen shared vans will drop you on the highway 1km from the ticket booth.

Cabs in town charge M$100 to the ruins.

It's about a 3.5km bike ride from the town center, with plenty of rentals available.

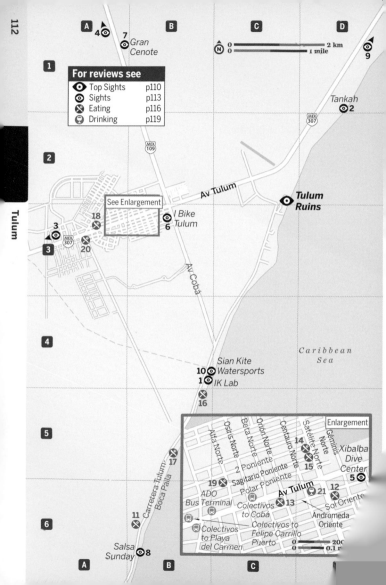

Sights

IK Lab
GALLERY

1  MAP P112, B4

In this mind-bending contemporary art gallery at Azulik resort, guests enter barefoot to interact with floors of polished cement and *bejuco* (vine-like wood) as living organisms. Opened by the great-grandson of art collector Peggy Guggenheim, the dreamlike exhibition space of meandering expanses was conceived so viewers could experience art alongside Tulum's natural elements, all under geometrically patterned wood domes.

An adjacent 12m dome, an impressive architectural feat built according to ancient geometric principles, can be viewed here as well, but by appointment only. (📞984-980-06-40; www.iklab.art; Carretera Tulum-Boca Paila Km 5; admission free; ⊘10am-noon)

Tankah
BEACH

2  MAP P112, D1

A few kilometers south of the Hwy 307 turnoff for Punta Solimán is the exit for Tankah, a picturesque stretch of beach and top-end accommodations that have the sea for a front yard and mangroves out back.

Uyo Ochel Maya
TOURS

3  MAP P112, A3

Tour Chunyaxche and Muyil lagoons by boat and swim in a centuries-old Maya canal. It's a lovely way to

Gran Cenote (p115)

see the second-largest lagoon in Quintana Roo, and the mangroves harbor orchids, saprophytes and numerous birds. To reach the lagoon shore by car, turn down a dirt road about 250m south of the Muyil archaeological site. (📱WhatsApp only 983-124-80-01; Muyil; adult M$700, parking M$50; ⏱8am-4pm)

Zacil-Ha
SWIMMING

4 ◉ MAP P112, A1

At this cenote you can combine swimming, snorkeling and ziplining. It's 8km west of Avenida Tulum on the road to Cobá. There's even a bar, too! (📱cell 984-2189029; www.facebook.com/cenotezacilha; Hwy 109 Km 8; admission M$80, snorkel gear M$30, zip-line M$10; ⏱10am-6pm)

Xibalba Dive Center
DIVING

5 ◉ MAP P112, D5

One of the best dive shops in Tulum, Xibalba is known for its safety-first approach to diving. The center specializes in cave and cavern diving, visiting sites such as Dos Ojos (p93) and the spooky **Cenote Angelita** (Hwy 307 Km 213; cenote dives M$300, snorkeling M$200; ⏱7am-5pm). Xibalba doubles as a hotel (rooms from US$100) and offers attractive packages combining lodging, diving trips and diving courses. (📱984-871-29-53; www.xibalbadivecenter.com; Andromeda Oriente 7, btwn Libra Sur & Géminis Sur; 1-/2-cavern dive incl gear US$90/150)

Diving in Parque Dos Ojos (p93)

JAN WLODARCZYK/ALAMY STOCK PHOTO ®

I Bike Tulum CYCLING

6 ◉ MAP P112, B3

Rents beach cruisers with lock and helmet, or, if you prefer, a scooter. (☏984-802-55-18; www.ibiketulum.com; Av Cobá Sur, btwn Sol Oriente & Gama Oriente; bicycle/scooter per day M$130/763; ⏲8:30am-5:30pm Mon-Sat)

Gran Cenote SWIMMING

7 ◉ MAP P112, A1

About 4km out of central Tulum, this is a worthwhile stop on the highway out to the Cobá ruins, especially if it's a hot day. You can snorkel among small fish and see underwater formations in the caverns if you bring your own scuba gear. A cab from Tulum costs M$100 one way (but check first to avoid surprises). (Hwy 109 s/n; admission M$180, snorkeling gear M$80, diving M$200; ⏲8:10am-4:45pm)

Salsa Sunday DANCING

8 ◉ MAP P112, B6

Take free salsa dancing lessons at 6:30pm at beachside hotel-restaurant La Zebra, then strut your stuff with live salsa music from 8pm to 11pm. It's a festive

Tulum's History

Most archaeologists believe that Tulum was occupied during the late post-Classic period (AD 1200–1521) and that it was an important port town during its heyday. The Maya sailed up and down this coast, maintaining trading routes all the way down into Belize. When Spanish conquistador Juan de Grijalva sailed past in 1518, he was amazed by the sight of the walled city, its buildings painted a gleaming red, blue and yellow and a ceremonial fire flaming atop its seaside watchtower.

The ramparts that surround three sides of Tulum (the fourth side being the sea) leave little question as to its strategic function as a fortress. Several meters thick and 3m to 5m high, the walls protected the city during a period of considerable strife between Maya city-states. Not all of Tulum was situated within the walls. The vast majority of the city's residents lived outside them; the civic-ceremonial buildings and palaces likely housed Tulum's ruling class.

The city was abandoned about 75 years after the Spanish conquest. It was one of the last of the ancient cities to be abandoned; most others had been given back to nature long before the arrival of the Spanish. But Maya pilgrims continued to visit over the years, and indigenous refugees from the War of the Castes took shelter here from time to time.

Sunday tradition in Tulum. (📱cell 984-1154726; www.lazebratulum.com; Carretera Tulum-Boca Paila Km 8.2, La Zebra; ⏰6:30-11pm Sun)

Cenote Manatí

SWIMMING

9 👁 MAP P112, D1

Named for the gentle 'sea cows' that used to frequent the beach, this is a beautiful series of seven cenotes connected by a channel that winds through mangroves a short distance before heading back underground briefly to reach the sea. The swimming, snorkeling and kayaking are great, though prices have shot up in recent years. (Tankah; admission M$120, snorkel tour M$500, 2-person kayak per hr M$250; ⏰8am-6pm)

Sian Kite Watersports

KITEBOARDING

10 👁 MAP P112, B4

Offers one-hour introductory kite-boarding lessons (if you can round up other people you'll save some pesos by paying a cheaper group rate). You can also take surfing classes here. It's at Papaya Playa Project, which is 3km southeast of the Avenida Tulum–Cobá intersection and about 500m south of the coast road T-junction. (📱WhatsApp only 984-185-11-51; www.facebook.com/siankitetulum; Carretera Tulum-Boca Paila Km 4.5, Papaya Playa Project hotel; surfing/kiteboarding lessons per hour M$40/80; ⏰9am-5pm)

Eating

Hartwood

FUSION $$$

11 🍴 MAP P112, B6

Assuming you can get in (accepts walk-ins and online reservations made one month in advance), this sweet 'n' simple nouveau cuisine restaurant down on the beach road will definitely impress. Ingredients are fresh and local, flavors and techniques are international. The chalkboard menu changes daily, and the solar-powered open kitchen and wood-burning oven serve to accentuate the delicious dishes.

It's about 4.5km south of the T-junction. Cash only. (www.hartwoodtulum.com; Carretera Tulum-Boca Paila Km 7.5; mains M$380-500; ⏰5:30-10pm Wed-Sun)

Taquería Honorio

TACOS $

12 🍴 MAP P112, D6

It began as a street stall and became such a hit that it's now a taco place with a proper roof over-head. Most folks go here for the *cochinita* (pulled pork in annatto marinade), served on handmade tortillas or in *tortas* (sandwiches). Also well worth seeking out here are Yucatecan classics such as *relleno negro* (shredded turkey in a chili-based dark sauce). (📱984-134-87-31; www.facebook.com/taqueria honorio; Satélite Sur; tacos M$16-22, tortas M$35-40; ⏰6am-2pm)

La Gloria de Don Pepe TAPAS $$

13 ✗ MAP P112, C6

With its 'A meal without wine is called breakfast' sign, this spot tickles the taste buds with delicious tapas plates and fine seafood paella. And wine – did we mention there's wine? A perfect place to come to talk to a friend for a couple of hours without being drowned out by noise. Alfresco seating is also possible. (📞cell 984-1524471; www.facebook.com/lagloriadedonpepe; Orión Sur, cnr Andromeda Oriente; tapas M$60-195; ⏱1:30-10:30pm Tue-Sun)

Azafran BREAKFAST $$

14 ✗ MAP P112, C5

A great little German-owned breakfast spot in a shady rear garden, the favorite dish is the 'hangover breakfast': a hearty portion of homemade sausage, mashed potatoes, eggs, rye toast and bacon – you might even have a lettuce sighting. There are lighter items on the menu, too, such as freshly baked bagels topped with brined salmon. Cash only. (📞cell 984-1296130; Av Satélite Norte s/n, cnr Calle 2 Poniente; mains M$75-125; ⏱8am-3pm Wed-Mon; 🌱)

Paradise Beach, Tulum

made cocktails that can be enjoyed immensely at sunset on the property's rear observation deck. Everything on the menu is prepared with a gourmet twist. The gravel floors, painted tables and chairs, and hookah decorations all add to the flair. (📞 cell 984-181-1152; www.facebook.com/purocorazon. tulum.1; Carretera Tulum-Boca Paila Km 5.5; mains M$160-350; 🕙 8am-10pm Tue-Sun; 🛜 🌱)

Posada Margherita   ITALIAN $$$

17 🍴 MAP P112, B5

This hotel's beachside restaurant is candlelit at night, making it a beautiful, romantic place to dine. The fantastic food, including pasta, is made fresh daily and consists mostly of organic ingredients. The wines and house mezcal are excellent. It's 3km south of the T-junction. Cash only. Parking can be a nightmare. (📞 WhatsApp only 984-801-84-93; www.posadamargherita. com; Carretera Tulum-Boca Paila Km 4.5; mains M$295-520; 🕙 7:30am-10pm)

Barracuda   SEAFOOD $$

18 🍴 MAP P112, A3

A very popular seafood eatery at the south end of the center, known for its *parillada de mariscos*, a large platter (for three people) with grilled fish, shrimp, crayfish, octopus and squid. (📞 984-160-03-25; www.facebook.com/barracuda tulum.qr; Av Tulum, cnr Luna Norte; mains M$90-180, seafood platter M$490; 🕙 9am-11pm; 🛜)

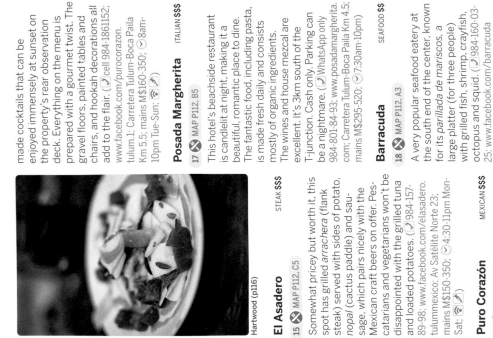

Hartwood (p116)

NICHOLAS GILL/ALAMY STOCK PHOTO ©

El Asadero   STEAK $$$

15 🍴 MAP P112, C5

Somewhat pricey but worth it, this spot has grilled *arrachera* (flank steak) served with sides of potato, *nopal* (cactus paddle) and sausage, which pairs nicely with the Mexican craft beers on offer. Pescatarians and vegetarians won't be disappointed with the grilled tuna and loaded potatoes. (📞 984-157-89-98; www.facebook.com/elasadero. tulummexico; Av Satélite Norte 23; mains M$150-350; 🕙 4:30-11pm Mon-Sat; 🛜 🌱)

Puro Corazón   MEXICAN $$$

16 🍴 MAP P112, B5

Reasonably priced (by Zona Hotelera standards), this inviting spot serves excellent house-

Le Bistro FRENCH $$

19 ✗ MAP P112, B6

Simple, elegantly prepared French food at excellent prices. Seafood features heavily on the menu but there are steaks, chicken and tasty baguettes to choose from, too. Meals and fresh-baked pastries are served in the restaurant-hotel's tastefully decorated lobby. (☏984-688-22-61; www.facebook.com/lebistro.tulum; Sagitario Poniente s/n, cnr Alfa Norte; mains M$100-180; ⏱7:30am-10pm Tue-Sun)

El Camello Jr SEAFOOD $$

20 ✗ MAP P112, A3

Immensely popular with locals, this roadside eatery guarantees fresh fish and seafood. Regulars don't even need to look at the menu – it's all about the mixed ceviche (seafood marinated in lemon or lime juice, garlic and seasonings), seafood soup or lobster, when in season. (☏984-871-20-36; www.facebook.com/restauranteelcamellojr; Av Tulum, cnr Av Kukulkán; mains M$100-165, lobster M$380-450; ⏱10:30am-10pm Thu-Tue; P)

Drinking

Batey BAR

21 ☺ MAP P112, D6

Mojitos sweetened with fresh-pressed cane sugar are the main

Sound Tulum 🎧

This two-week-long **music festival** (www.soundtulum.com; ⏱late Dec-early Jan) draws top international names in the underground electronic music scene. See website for lineup, venues and tickets.

attraction at this popular Cuban bar, with fun music acts in the rear garden. Most nights the crowd spills into the street, while inside cane is pressed on top of an iconic painted VW bug. (☏cell 984-7454571; www.facebook.com/batey tulum; Centauro Sur 7, btwn Av Tulum & Andromeda Oriente; ⏱8am-1:30am Mon-Sat, 4:30pm-1am Sun)

Papaya Playa Project BAR

Trendy hotel Papaya Playa Project (see **10** ◎ Map p112, B4) hosts monthly full-moon parties and Saturday DJ nights with resident and guest spinsters at its beachside club. It's 500m south of the T-junction. There's usually a cover charge. (☏984-871-11-60; www.facebook.com/papayaplayaproject; Carretera Tulum-Boca Paila Km 4.5; ⏱10pm-3am Sat)

Worth a Trip 🔭
Cobá

Cobá's ruins are a treat and exploring them is the main reason for coming here: the state's tallest pyramid, a beautiful ball court and a variety of other structures make for a fun few hours. The village is quiet and cute, with a croc-filled lagoon, some cenotes and a growing number of hotels and restaurants...but people mostly come for the ruins.

www.inah.gob.mx

admission M$70, guides M$600-650

🕘 8am-4:30pm

Grupo Cobá

The most prominent structure in the Grupo Cobá is La Iglesia (The Church). It's an enormous pyramid; if you were allowed to climb it, you could see the surrounding lakes (which look lovely on a clear day) and the Nohoch Mul pyramid. To reach it walk just under 100m along the main path from the entrance and turn right.

Take the time to explore Grupo Cobá; it has a couple of corbeled-vault passages you can walk through. Near its northern edge, on the way back to the main path and the bicycle concession, is a very well-restored *juego de pelota* (ball court).

Grupo Macanxoc

Grupo Macanxoc is notable for its numerous restored stelae, some of which are believed to depict reliefs of royal women who are thought to have come from Tikal. Though many are worn down by the elements, a number of them are still in good condition and are worth a detour.

Grupo de las Pinturas

The temple at Grupo de las Pinturas (Paintings Group) bears traces of glyphs and frescoes above its door and remnants of richly colored plaster inside. You approach the temple from the southeast. Leave by the trail at the northwest (opposite the temple steps) to see two stelae. The first of these is 20m along, beneath a *palapa*. Here, a regal figure stands over two others, one of them kneeling with his hands bound behind him. Sacrificial captives lie beneath the feet of a ruler at the base. You'll need to use your imagination, as this and most of the other stelae here are quite worn. Continue along the path past another badly weathered and a small temple to rejoin a path leading the next group of structures.

★ Top Tips

● Arrive before 11am to beat literally hundreds of other people coming in from Cancún, Playa and Tulum.

● From a sustainable-tourism perspective, it's great to stay the night in small communities like Cobá, but don't plan on staying up late.

✕ Take a Break

At the end of the town's main drag, by the lake, **Restaurant La Pirámide** (☏984-206-71-75, 984-206-70-18; Av Principal s/n; mains M$105-170, buffet M$180; ◷8am-5pm; 🛜) is touristy but does decent Yucatecan fare, or you can opt for the lunch buffet between noon and 3pm.

★ Getting There

Most buses serving Cobá swing down to the ruins to drop off passengers at a small bus stop, but you can also get off in town.

Getting Around

In addition to the ruins, the area has several cenotes south of town. If you **rent a bike** (near ruins bus stop; bikes per day M$50; ⏱10am-5pm) it makes a nice ride. Otherwise, you'll need to find your own way to get there.

Grupo Nohoch Mul

Nohoch Mul (Big Mound) is also known as the Great Pyramid (which sounds a lot better than Big Mound). It reaches a height of 42m, making it the second-tallest Maya structure on the Yucatán Peninsula (Calakmul's Estructura II, at 45m, is the tallest). Climbing the old steps can be scary for some. Two diving gods are carved over the doorway of the temple at the top (built in the post-Classic period, AD 1100–1521), similar to sculptures at Tulum.

The view from up top is over many square kilometers of flat scrubby forest, with peeks of lake.

Juego de Pelota

An impressive ball court, one of several in the ruins. Don't miss the relief of a jaguar and the skull-like carving in the center of the court.

Xaibé

This is a tidy, semicircular stepped building, almost fully restored. Its name means 'the Crossroads,' as it

History

Cobá was settled earlier than Chichén Itzá or Tulum, and construction reached its peak between AD 800 and 1000. Archaeologists believe that this city once covered 70 sq km and held some 40,000 Maya.

Cobá's architecture is a mystery; its towering pyramids and stelae resemble the architecture of Tikal, which is several hundred kilometers away, rather than the much nearer sites of Chichén Itzá and the northern Yucatán Peninsula.

Archaeologists say they now know that between AD 200 and 600, when Cobá had control over a vast territory of the peninsula, alliances with Tikal were made through military and marriage arrangements in order to facilitate trade between the Guatemalan and Yucatecan Maya. Stelae appear to depict female rulers from Tikal holding ceremonial bars and flaunting their power by standing on captives. These Tikal royal females, when married to Cobá's royalty, may have brought architects and artisans with them.

Archaeologists are still baffled by the extensive network of *sacbeob* (ceremonial limestone avenues or paths between great Maya cities) in this region, with Cobá as the hub. The longest runs nearly 100km west from the base of Cobá's great Nohoch Mul pyramid to the Maya settlement of Yaxuna. In all, some 40 *sacbeob* passed through Cobá, parts of the huge astronomical 'time machine' that was evident in every Maya city.

The first excavation at Cobá was led by the Austrian archaeologist Teobert Maler in 1891. There was little subsequent investigation until 1926, when the Carnegie Institute financed the first of two expeditions led by Sir J Eric S Thompson and Harry Pollock. After their 1930 expedition, not much happened until 1973, when the Mexican government began to finance excavation. Archaeologists now estimate that Cobá contains more than 6500 structures, of which just a few have been excavated and restored, though work is ongoing.

marks the juncture of four separate *sacbeob* (ceremonial limestone avenues or paths between great Maya cities).

Templo 10

Here you can see an exquisitely carved stela (AD 730) depicting a ruler standing imperiously over two captives.

Explore ✦

Isla Cozumel

Fascinating for its dual personality, Cozumel offers an odd mix – quietly authentic neighborhoods existing alongside tourist-friendly playgrounds. Leaving the tourist area behind, you'll find garages that still have shrines to the Virgin and a spirited Caribbean energy in the air. And, of course, there are epic experiences to be had, such as diving at some of the best reefs in the world.

The Short List

○ **Dive Sites (p127)** *Plunging into the blue and exploring world-class sites with a top dive shop.*

○ **Parque Punta Sur (p132)** *Escaping to a quiet beach with lagoon boat tours, fine snorkeling and wildlife-watching opportunities.*

○ **Turquoise Beach Bar (p139)** *Taking in a sunset over drinks and music alongside a resident pig with a hearty appetite.*

○ **El Cielo (p132)** *Swimming at a beach with shallow waters and encountering undersea wildlife.*

Getting There & Away

🛳 Most people arrive by ferry, but there's a small airport as well.

🚌 Bus tickets for onward travel in the Yucatán can be purchased in Cozumel, but you actually board the bus in Playa del Carmen and continue from there. You can buy tickets in advance at **ADO Ticket Office** (Map p130, E7; 📞 987-869-25-53; Calle 2 Norte s/n, btwn Avs 5 Norte & 10 Norte; 🕐 8am-9pm Mon-Fri, 9:30am-7pm Sat & Sun).

Isla Cozumel Map on p130

Top Sight 📷
Diving Isla Cozumel

A visit to Cozumel wouldn't be complete without some diving action – the reefs here are among the world's best. Diving buffs will want to devote several days to these otherworldly sites, which have fantastic year-round visibility (commonly 30m or more) and a jaw-droppingly impressive variety of marine life, including rays, eels, groupers, barracudas, turtles, sharks, coral and huge sponges.

Diving Basics

There are scores of dive operators on Cozumel. All limit the size of their groups to six or eight divers, and the good ones take pains to match up divers of similar skill levels. Some offer snorkeling and deep-sea fishing trips as well as diving instruction.

Prices are usually quoted in US dollars. In general, expect to pay anywhere between US$100 and US$115 for a two-tank dive (equipment included) or an introductory 'resort' course. PADI open-water certification costs from US$350 to US$420. Multiple-dive packages and discounts for groups or those paying in cash can bring rates down significantly.

If you encounter a decompression emergency, head immediately to the hyperbaric chamber at **Cozumel International Hospital** (Map p130, D8; ☑ 987-872 14 30; www.hospitalcoz umel.com; Calle 5 Sur 21B, btwn Avs Melgar & 5 Sur; ☺24hr).

If diving is your primary goal, you may want to time your trip for September or October, when weather conditions are ideal. Severe weather can affect turbidity and prevent the boats from leaving, among other hassles.

Diving Sites

With more than 60 surrounding reefs, excellent visibility and an abundance of marine life, it's no wonder the late, great oceanographer Jacques Cousteau called Cozumel one of the world's top diving destinations. Among the island's many great sites you'll find everything from challenging wall dives to shallow snorkeling spots.

Santa Rosa Wall

This is the biggest of the famous dive sites. The wall is so large most people are able to see only a third of it on one tank. Regardless of where you're dropped, expect to find enormous overhangs and tunnels covered with corals and sponges. Stoplight parrotfish, black grouper

★ **Top Tips**

○ The island can have strong currents (sometimes around 3 knots), making drift dives the standard.

○ Evaluate conditions and plan your route carefully, selecting an exit point down-current beforehand, then staying alert for shifts in currents.

○ Keep an eye out (and your ears open) for boat traffic.

★ **Recommended Diving Operators**

Deep Blue (p129) Features knowledge-able staff, state-of-the-art gear and fast boats.

Aldora Divers (☑ 987-872-33-97; www.aldora.com; Calle 5 Sur 37; 1-/2-tank dives incl equipment US$66/113, 3-tank shark-cave dives US$232; ☺7am-3pm & 6-8pm) One of the best dive shops on Cozumel; takes divers to the windward side of the island when weather is bad on the western side.

and barracuda hang out here. The average visibility is 30m and minimum depth 10m, with an average closer to 25m. Carry a flashlight with you, even if you're diving at noon, as it will help to bring out the color of the coral at depth and illuminate the critters hiding in crevices. Hurricane Wilma in 2005 left shallower spots with uncovered coral, but for the most part it is unharmed.

Punta Sur Reef
Unforgettable for its coral caverns, each of which is named, this reef is for very experienced divers only. Before you dive be sure to ask your divemaster to point out the Devil's Throat. This cave opens into a cathedral room with four tunnels, all of which make for some pretty hairy exploration. Only certified cave divers should consider entering the Devil's Throat. Butterfly fish, angelfish and whip corals abound at the reef.

Colombia Shallows
Also known as Colombia Gardens, Colombia Shallows lends itself equally well to snorkeling and scuba diving. Because it's a shallow dive (maximum depth 10m, average 2m to 4m), its massive coral buttresses covered with sponges and other resplendent life forms are well illuminated.

The current at Colombia Gardens is generally light to moderate. This and the shallow water allow you to spend hours here if you want; it's impossible to become bored spying all the elkhorn coral, pillar coral and anemones that live here.

Snorkeling

The best snorkeling sites are reached by boat. Most snorkeling-only outfits located downtown go to one of three stretches of reef nearby, all accessible from the beach. If you go with a dive outfit instead, you can often get to better spots, such as Palancar Reef or the adjacent Colombia Shallows, near the island's southern end.

Your best option is to head out on a diving boat with **Deep Blue** (Map p130, E8; ☎987-872-56-53; www.deepbluecozumel.com; Salas 200; 2-tank dives incl equipment US$100, snorkeling incl gear US$60; ⏱7am-9pm), which will take you to three of the finest snorkeling sites on the island.

You can save on boat fares (though you will see fewer fish) by walking into the gentle surf north of town. One good spot is beach club **Buccanos** (Map p130, C2; ☎987-872-01-00; www.buccanos.com; Carretera San Juan Km 4.5; snorkeling incl gear US$20; ⏱9am-4:30pm), next to Hotel Playa Azul, 4km north of the turnoff to the airport. Its *palapas* offer shade, and it has a swimming area with a sheltering wharf and a small artificial reef.

It's best not to snorkel alone away from the beach area. Even when snorkeling right from the beach you need to be mindful of boat traffic, and always keep an eye on conditions.

As with diving the ideal time for snorkeling is September or October, when the weather and conditions are at their best.

Palancar Gardens

This dive consists of a strip reef about 25m wide and very long, riddled with fissures and tunnels. The major features are enormous stovepipe sponges and vivid yellow tube sponges, and you can always find damselfish, parrotfish and angelfish around you. In the deeper parts of the reef, divers will want to keep an eye out for the lovely black corals.

Maracaibo

One of Cozumel's least visited sites, Maracaibo is the island's southernmost reef, known as a spectacular yet challenging wall dive. It's for experienced divers only – you'll be plunging to depths of 40m in waters with strong currents. Common marine life sightings include turtles, spotted eagle rays, nurse sharks and blacktip reef sharks.

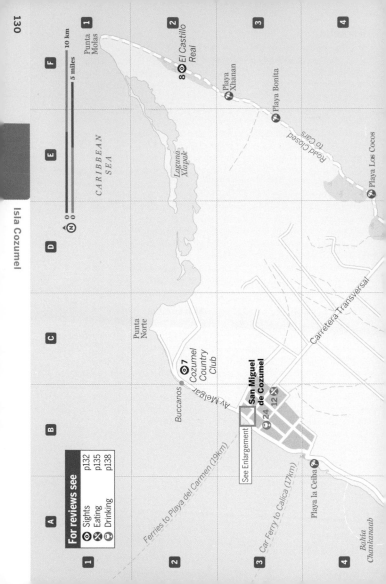

Isla Cozumel

For reviews see

◉ Sights	p132
✖ Eating	p135
🅑 Drinking	p138

CARIBBEAN SEA

Punta Molas

8 ◉ El Castillo Real

Playa Xhanan

Playa Bonita

Road Closed To Cars

Playa Los Cocos

Laguna Xlapak

Punta Norte

Cozumel Country Club

◉ 7

Buccanos

Av Melgar

See Enlargement

San Miguel de Cozumel

🅑 1

24 ✖

12 ✖

Carretera Transversal

Ferries to Playa del Carmen (19km)

Car Ferry to Calica (17km)

Playa la Ceiba 🅑

Bahía Chankanaab

5 miles

10 km

N

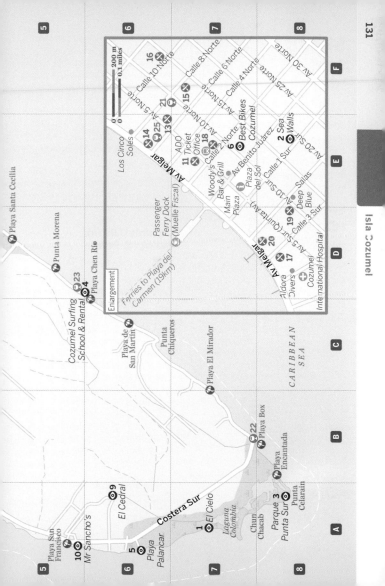

CARIBBEAN SEA

Enlargement

Ferries to Playa del
Carmen (19km)

Passenger
Ferry Dock
(Muelle Fiscal)

Los Cinco
Soles

16

Calle 10 Norte

Calle 8 Norte

Calle 6 Norte

Calle 4 Norte

21

25   14

13

15

11 ADO
Ticket
Office

18

6

Best Bikes
Cozumel

2 Sea
Walls

Av 5 Norte

Av 10 Norte

Av 15 Norte

Av 25 Norte

Av 30 Norte

Av Melgar

Woody's
Bar & Grill

Calle 2
Av Benito Juárez

Plaza
del Sol

Main
Plaza

Calle 1 Sur

Av 5 Sur (Quinta Av)

Av 10 Sur

Av 20 Sur

19

Deep
Blue

Calle 3

Salas

20

17

Av Melgar

Aldora
Divers

Cozumel
International Hospital

200 m
0.1 miles

0
0

Playa Santa Cecilia

Punta Morena

23 4

Playa Chen Río

Cozumel Surfing
School & Rental

Playa de
San Martín

Punta
Chiqueros

Playa El Mirador

Playa Box

22 Playa Encantada

Playa San
Francisco

10 Mr Sancho's

9

El Cedral

5 Playa
Palancar

Costera Sur

1 El Cielo

Laguna
Colombia

Chun
Chacab

Parque 3
Punta Sur

Punta
Celaraín

Sights

El Cielo   BEACH

1 ◉ MAP P130, A7

Living up to its heavenly name, El Cielo's shallow turquoise waters are ideal for snorkeling and swimming among starfish, stingrays and small fish. Located on the island's southwest side, it's only accessible by boat but all the dive shops make trips there.

Sea Walls   PUBLIC ART

2 ◉ MAP P130, E8

Local and international artists backed by the PangeaSeed foundation created 36 large-scale public murals in 2015 to raise awareness about ocean conservation and responsible coastal development. A DIY walking tour reveals cool downtown works like a towering sea-monster mural on Calle 1 Sur and Avenida 20 Sur. Ask the **tourist office** (Map p130, E7; ☎987-869-02-12; www.cozumel. travel; Av 5 Sur s/n, Plaza del Sol, 2nd fl; ⊗8am-3pm Mon-Fri) for a printed map of the murals. (www.pangea seed.foundation/cozumel-mexico; San Miguel de Cozumel)

Parque Punta Sur   NATURE RESERVE

3 ◉ MAP P130, A8

For the price of admission to this park, you can visit a lighthouse, a small nautical museum and a Maya ruin. The park road leads past an observation tower from where it's possible to spot migratory birds and, occasionally, crocodiles, and continuing further west you'll reach a beach area with a shallow reef, a restaurant and boat tours (noon, 1pm and 2pm) to Laguna Colombia. You'll need your own vehicle or a taxi (M$300 one way) to get here. (☎987-872-40-14, cell 987-8761303; www.cozumelparks. com; Carretera Costera Sur Km 27; adult/child 4-12yr US$14/8; ⊗9am-4pm Mon-Sat)

Cozumel Surfing School & Rental   SURFING

4 ◉ MAP P130, D5

Hit the surf with Nacho Gutierrez (who is rocking the Johnny Depp look in a serious way). You'll find Nacho at **El Pescador** restaurant (Km 42.9) on Playa Chen Río. He usually holds surfing classes at Punta Chiqueros, where you can rent boards at **Playa Bonita** restaurant (Km 37). Reserve ahead for surfing lessons. Nacho also runs spear-fishing outings. (☎USA 612-287-5549, cell 987-1119290; www. cozumelsurfing.com; Carretera Coastal Oriente Km 42.9, Playa Chen Río; surfboard per day US$30-40, surfing class US$110, spear-fishing trip US$80)

Playa Palancar   BEACH

5 ◉ MAP P130, A6

About 17km south of San Miguel, Palancar is a great beach to visit during the week when the crowds thin out. It has a beach club renting snorkel gear (US$10) and there's a restaurant. Nearby, Arrecife Palancar (Palancar Reef) has some excellent diving (it's known as Palancar Gardens), and fine snorkeling (Palancar Shallows).

A dive shop here runs snorkeling and diving trips to nearby sites. (☎cell 987-1185154; www.buceopalancar.com.mx; Carretera Costera Sur Km 19.5; ⏱9am-5pm)

Best Bikes Cozumel   CYCLING

6 ◉ MAP P130, E7

A good selection of beach cruisers, mountain bikes and hybrids. (☎cell 987-1260503; www.bestbikes cozumel.com; Av 10 Norte 14; per hr/day from M$30/150; ⏱9am-6pm)

Cozumel Country Club   GOLF

7 ◉ MAP P130, C2

This 18-hole, Nicklaus-designed course is a challenging one, and crocodiles inhabit all its water features, so keep yourself at least several club lengths from their jaws. The grounds are designated as a certified Audubon sanctuary and you can book early-morning bird-watching tours led by an English-speaking biologist. (☎987-872-95-70; www.cozumelcountryclub.com.mx; off Carretera Costera Norte; rates incl cart US$89-125, bird-watching tour US$50; ⏱tee times 6:30am-3pm)

Parque Punta Sur

Punta Molas

If you'd like to explore the island's wild and undeveloped side, beyond where the east-coast highway meets the Carretera Transversal, the best bet is to arrange an off-road tour with **Omar's Island Buggy Tours** (✆cell 987-1055892; www.omarsislandbuggytours.com; tours per person US$130). Escapists will enjoy venturing out to this remote area, where you can snorkel at secluded beaches and visit small Maya ruins and a deserted lighthouse at the northernmost point.

Only off-road vehicles can handle the difficult dirt road and a fallen sign at the entrance reads: 'Enter at your own risk. Irregular path even for 4x4 vehicles.' The truth is, it's tough to even find a place to rent an ATV. If you do head up the road, be aware that you can't count on flagging down another motorist for help in the event of a breakdown or accident, and most car-rental agencies' insurance policies don't cover any mishaps on unpaved roads. In other words, even if you can find someone willing to rent you a vehicle for Punta Molas, you're on your own.

About 17km up the road are the hard-to-find Maya ruins known as El Castillo Real and, a few kilometers further north, **Aguada Grande**. Both sites are only accessible on foot. In the vicinity of Punta Molas are some fairly good beaches and a few more minor ruins.

El Castillo Real   ARCHAEOLOGICAL SITE

8 ◉ MAP P130, F2

Down the same intimidating, 4WD-only road that leads to Punta Molas are the large Maya ruins known as El Castillo Real (The Royal Castle). The archaeological site, as well as the Aguada Grande ruins a few kilometers' hike away, are both quite far gone, their significance having blown off into the breeze some time ago. Still, half the fun is in getting there, right? (admission free; ⏱8am-5pm)

El Cedral   ARCHAEOLOGICAL SITE

9 ◉ MAP P130, A6

This Maya ruin, a fertility temple, is the oldest on the island. It's the size of a small house and has no ornamentation. El Cedral is thought to have been an important ceremonial site; the small church standing next to the tiny ruin today is evidence that the site still has religious significance for locals. (admission per vehicle M$35; ⏱24hr)

Mr Sancho's
HORSEBACK RIDING

10 ◎ MAP P130, A5

Saddle up at Mr Sancho's for guided horseback rides along the coast and into the surrounding jungle, where you can trot through a mangrove-lined beach and see wildlife. Be sure to wear clothing appropriate for a horseback ride. Closed-toe shoes are especially recommended. (☎987-120-22-20, cell 987-8719174; www.mrsanchos.com; Carretera Costera Sur Km 15; 30min rides US$35; ⊙8am-5pm Mon-Sat)

Eating

Kinta
CONTEMPORARY MEXICAN $$$

11 ✖ MAP P130, E7

Putting a gourmet twist on Mexican classics, this chic bistro is one of the best restaurants on the island. The Midnight Pork Ribs are a tried-and-true favorite, while the wood-fired oven turns out spectacular oven-baked fish. For dessert treat yourself to a *budín de la abuelita*, aka 'granny's pudding.' (☎987-869-05-44; www.kintares taurante.com; Av 5 Norte 148; mains M$260-340; ⊙5-11pm; 🛜)

Camarón Dorado
SEAFOOD $

12 ✖ MAP P130, B3

If you're headed to the windward side of the island or just want to see a different aspect of Cozumel, drop by the Camarón Dorado for a bite, assuming you're early enough. Be warned: the *camarón empanizado* (breaded shrimp) tor-

tas and tacos are highly addictive. It's 2.5km southeast of the passenger ferry terminal. (☎987-872-72-87, cell 987-1181281; www.facebook.com/camaron.dorado; cnr Av Juárez & Calle 105 Sur; tacos M$18-35, tortas M$29-55; ⊙7am-1:30pm Tue-Sun; 🛜)

'Ohana
PIZZA $$$

13 ✖ MAP P130, E6

Known for its Chicago-style deep-dish pizza and friendly neighborhood expat bar, 'Ohana (meaning family in Hawaiian) definitely feels like home. The owner Matt (a Windy City transplant) knows a thing or two about making a proper pizza pie and he mixes his own mezcal and tequila cream liqueurs, which are fine if you like booze that tastes like dessert.

FOTOS593/SHUTTERSTOCK ©

Shopping 🛍️

Like many shops along Avenida Melgar, **Los Cinco Soles** (Map p130, E6; ☎987-872-90-04; www.loscincosoles.com; Av Melgar 27; ⏰8am-8pm Mon-Fri, from 9am Sat, 10am-6pm Sun) sells its fair share of kitsch. However, there are some keepers on the shelves if you take the time to look, such as black ceramics from Oaxaca, Talavera pottery and colorful Day of the Dead skeleton dioramas.

(☎cell 987-5641771; www.ohana cozumel.com; Av 5 Norte 341; pizzas M$250; ⏰5-11pm Mon-Sat)

Guido's Restaurant   ITALIAN $$$

14 🍴 MAP P130, E6

Drawing on recipes handed down from her father, Guido, chef Yvonne Villiger has created a menu ranging from wood-fired pizzas and homemade pastas to prosciutto-wrapped scallops. To accompany the meal, order a pitcher of sangria, the house specialty. The cocktail menu is equally impressive; there is even house-made tonic syrup for your G&Ts. (☎987-869-25-89; www.guidos cozumel.com; Av Melgar 23; mains M$210-345, pizzas M$205-275; ⏰11am-11pm Mon-Sat, from 3pm Sun; 🛜)

La Cocay   MEDITERRANEAN $$

15 🍴 MAP P130, F7

Operating since 1996, this restaurant makes for a fancy night out, with an intimate, candlelit atmosphere and excellent food. Service can occasionally be slow, so plan to take your time. The menu changes seasonally but focuses on light, Mediterranean-influenced fare. It's also a good spot to grab drinks. (☎987-872-55-33; www. lacocay.com; Calle 8 Norte 208; mains M$120-330; ⏰5:30-11pm; 🛜)

Diez Con Quince   BREAKFAST $

16 🍴 MAP P130, F6

Mexican and gringo-friendly breakfasts such as eggs Benedict are served in a peaceful rear garden at this affordable restaurant. The menu also includes a fair share of vegetarian and vegan dishes, including Gouda-filled fried plantain patties and a superfood bowl packed with a dozen nutritious ingredients. (☎987-869-12-05; www. facebook.com/pg/diezconquince; Calle 10 Norte s/n, cnr Av 15 Norte; mains M$74-113; ⏰8am-5pm Mon-Wed & Sun, to 11pm Thu-Sat; 🛜🍴)

El Coffee Cozumel   CAFE $

17 🍴 MAP P130, D8

A tempting array of fresh-baked goods and organic coffee from the Mexican highlands make this place popular with locals and visitors alike. Pies are made daily, and it does a mean iced latte – perfect if you need to beat the heat. (📞987-869-04-56; coffeecozumel@gmail.com; Calle 3 Sur 98; mains M$60-89; ⊙7am-11pm; 🛜📶)

Taquería El Sitio   TACOS $

18 🍴 MAP P130, E7

For something quick, cheap and tasty, head over to El Sitio for breaded shrimp and fish tacos or a *huevo con chaya torta* (egg and tree-spinach sandwich). The folding chairs and concrete floor are nothing fancy, but the food is good. (Calle 2 Norte 124; tacos & tortas M$14-38; ⊙7:30am-12:30pm)

La Choza   MEXICAN $$

19 🍴 MAP P130, D8

An excellent and popular restaurant with a garden at the back, La Choza offers regional Mexican cuisine, with classics like chicken in *mole poblano* (a sauce of chilies, fruits, nuts, spices and chocolate). All mains come with soup. There's a *comida corrida* (set menu) for the lunch crowd. Don't miss the coffee brewed with cinnamon. Yum! (📞987-872-09-58; www.facebook.com/lachozaczm; Av 10 Sur 216; mains M$63-221, comida corrida M$171; ⊙7am-10pm; 🛜)

Tacos

Pepe's Grill
STEAK $$$

20 🍴 MAP P130, D8

This is traditionally considered Cozumel's finest restaurant and the prices reflect its reputation. The menu focuses mainly on Angus steaks, pastas, fresh fish and charbroiled lobster (available at market prices). (☎987-872-02-13; www.pepescozumel.com; Av Melgar 201; mains M$220-525; ⊙10am-11pm; 🛜)

Drinking

El Fish
BAR

21 🍺 MAP P130, F6

For the classic Cozumel *botana* bar experience (free snacks come to the table each time you order a new round), hit this fan-cooled establishment for a cold beer, tasty grub and a few laughs with the crowd of locals sitting around the semicircular bar. The kitchen closes at 7pm. (Calle 8 Norte s/n, cnr Av 10 Norte; ⊙noon-10pm)

Freedom in Paradise
BAR

22 🍺 MAP P130, B7

As much a viewing point as it is a great place for a chilled beer, reggae-themed Freedom in Paradise is a family-run endeavor that's been around for decades. The mellow *palapa* couldn't be a nicer spot to enjoy the vista. Across the street its sister location offers flavored-mezcal tastings. Long live Bob! (☎cell 987-5649164; www.bobmarleybar.com; Carretera Coastal Oriente Km 29.5; ⊙10am-6pm)

MIKOLAJN/ALAMY STOCK PHOTO ©

Coconuts Bar & Grill   BAR

23 ⊙ MAP P130, D5

'Coconuts' is used here metaphorically, and some of the decorations are a bit tacky (the thong-wearing beach balls, for instance), but what would you expect from a cliffside bar serving tropical drinks with Jimmy Buffett tunes in the background? The view can't be beat, and on a hot day the beer can't be beat either. Cash only. (☎ cell 987-1077110; www.coconutscozumel.com; Carretera Coastal Oriente Km 43.3; ⊙10am-7pm)

El Volado   BAR

24 ⊙ MAP P130, B3

This two-story Mexican pub is a good spot to brush up on your Spanish, as locals outnumber the tourists most nights. It's a fun, even refreshing, change from the tourist zone. (www.elvolado.com; cnr Av 20 Sur & Calle 15 Sur; ⊙7:30pm-2am Wed & Thu, to 3am Fri & Sat)

Aqua   BAR

25 ⊙ MAP P130, E6

The Hotel Flamingo's lobby bar is an attractive lounge drawing

Live Music

At **Turquoise Beach Bar** (☎ cell 987-1155057; www.facebook.com/turquoisecozumel beachclub; Av Melgar Km 2.8; ⊙9am-8pm Mon-Sat, 10am-11pm Sun), some surprisingly good rock cover bands play fun sunset shows several times a week. If you get tired of the beer routine, order a cocktail or potent mezcal. A festively plump pet pig named Taluhla roams the beach here for table scraps and she seems to be making out quite well.

There's also decent live music at **Woody's Bar & Grill** (Map p130, E7; www.cozumelradio.wixsite.com/woodys; Av Juárez s/n, btwn Avs 5 & 10; ⊙10am-midnight Mon-Fri, to 1am Sat & Sun; 🛜).

mostly an older, margarita-drinking expat crowd. (☎987-872-12-64; www.hotelflamingo.com; Calle 6 Norte 81; ⊙7am-11pm; 🛜)

Isla Cozumel Drinking

Worth a Trip 🔭
Reserva de la Biosfera Sian Ka'an

A sprawling jungle with a pristine coastline and camping sites for intrepid travelers, Sian Ka'an is home to a small population of spider and howler monkeys, American crocodiles, Central American tapirs, four turtle species, giant land crabs, more than 330 bird species (including roseate spoonbills and some flamingos), manatees and some 400 fish species, plus a wide array of plant life.

Sian Ka'an Biosphere Reserve

M$35

🕐 sunrise-sunset

Hiking & Camping

There are no hiking trails through the heart of the reserve; it's best explored with a professional guide.

For remote coastal camping, this is where intrepid adventuring really takes off. Bring a tent, a couple of hammocks, lots of water, mosquito nets and food supplies. Around 30km from the entrance gate is an excellent camping spot with the lagoon on one side and glorious blue ocean on the other.

Rough Road

The road can be a real muffler-buster between gradings, especially when holes are filled with water from recent rains, making it difficult to gauge their depth.

The southern half, south of the bridge beyond Boca Paila, is the worst stretch – some spots require experienced off-road handling or you'll sink into the mud. It is doable even in a non-4WD vehicle, but bring along a shovel and boards just in case – you can always stuff palm fronds under the wheels to gain traction – and plan on returning that rental with a lot more play in the steering wheel.

Community Tours Sian Ka'an

This sustainable-tourism project (cell 984-1140750, 984-871-22-02; www.siankaantours.org Osiris Sur, cnr Sol Oriente; tours per person US$85-125; 7am-9pm) is run by locals from Maya communities, and offers various excursions to the biosphere reserve. These include bird-watching tours, visiting Maya ruins, swimming in an ancient canal and kayaking.

★ **Top Tips**

o At the entrance gate, about 10km south of Tulum, there's a short nature trail that takes you to a rather nondescript cenote (Ben Ha); it's worth a quick look.

o About 8km south of the reserve entrance is a modest visitor area, a pull-off where you'll find a watchtower that provides tremendous bird's-eye views of the lagoon.

★ **Getting There**

Colectivos (M$15) run frequently between the biosphere reserve and Tulum. Pick one up on the corner of Venus Oriente and Orión Sur between 6am and 7:30pm.

Survival Guide

Playa del Carmen (p91) PHORTUN/SHUTTERSTOCK ©

Before You Go

Book Your Stay

o While it's easy to think the Riviera Maya is entirely top-end type lodging, there are plenty of hostels and lower-cost places too, making it doable for those on a tight budget.

o Cancún has a variety of accommodations ranging from budget to mind- and budget-blowing.

o Almost all hotels offer discounts during 'low' season, but many have up to five different rate periods. Christmas and New Year are always at a premium.

o Many places have great online promotions.

Useful Websites

Visit Mexico (www. visitmexico.com) Offers discounted rates on hotels for all budget ranges.

Cancun.com (www. cancun.com) For booking hotels, apartments and condos.

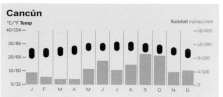

Cancún

When to Go

o **Apr–May** A visit to Cancún after the spring break dust settles offers a quieter side of the resort city (and great online deals)

o **Oct–Nov** Playa del Carmen hosts a wild Halloween street bash, then stick around for colorful Day of the Dead festivities in the Riviera Maya.

o **Dec–Jan** Underground electronic music event Sound Tulum features gigs at venues around Tulum and the party goes nonstop for two weeks.

Lonely Planet (www. lonelyplanet.com/ mexico/cancun/hotels) Recommendations and bookings.

Best Budget

Mayan Monkey
(998-217-53-32; www. mayanmonkey.com; Av Náder 32, Cancún Centro; dm/r incl breakfast & dinner from US$17/83; ⊝ 🌸 🛜 🛋; 🚉 R-1) Impeccably clean hostel serving two free meals a day and has a great rooftop pool.

Mezcal Hostel
(998-255-28-44; www. mezcalhostel.com; Mero 12,

Cancún Centro; dm/r incl breakfast & dinner from US$14/65; ⊝ 🌸 🛜 🛋; 🚉 R-1) Occupies a lovely two-story house with a swimming pool in the courtyard.

Los Girasoles (998-887-39-90; www.losgira solescancun.com.mx; Piña 20, Cancún Centro; r from M$600; ⊝ 🌸 @ 🛜) Centrally located downtown budget option offering clean rooms and a friendly staff.

Poc-Na Hostel (998-877-00-90; www.pocna. com; Matamoros 15, Isla Mujeres; dm/d incl breakfast from M$300/600;

⊖ ❋ 🛜) Seafront Isla Mujeres hostel with a superb beach bar.

El Jardín de Frida

(📞 984-871-28-16; www.fridastulum.com; Av Tulum, btwn Av Kukulkán & Chemuyil, Tulum; dm M$200-250, d/ste M$1000/1300; P ⊖ 🛜) Tulum eco-hostel decked out with Mexican pop art.

Best Midrange

Náder Hotel & Suites

(📞 998-884-15-84; www.suitesnadercancun.com; Av Náder 5, Cancún Centro; d/ste incl breakfast US$54/75; ⊖ ❋ 🛜; 🚭 R-1) Spacious family-friendly suites fitted with kitchens and comfy sitting areas.

Hotel Antillano

(📞 998-884-11-32; www.hotelantillano.com.mx; Claveles 1, Cancún Centro; d M$1200; P ⊖ ❋ 🛜 ☒; 🚭 R-1) Pleasant old-school downtown hotel within walking distance of cultural venue Parque de las Palapas.

Soberanis Hotel

(📞 998-884-45-64; www.soberanis.mx; Av Cobá 5 s/n, Cancún Centro; d from M$825; ⊖ @ 🛜; 🚭 R-1) Convenient location

near bus stop to the beach and there's a supermarket next door.

Hotel Maria Maria

(📞 983-834-21-16; www.facebook.com/hotelmariamaria; Av 3 No 600, cnr Calle 14, Laguna Bacalar; r M$950-1050, ste M$1150; P ⊖ ❋ 🛜) Well-run Laguna Bacalar hotel with tasteful suites and lagoon views, and two cheaper rooms on the ground floor.

Hotel Kin-Ha

(📞 984-871-23-21; www.hotelkinha.com; Orión Sur s/n, btwn Sol Oriente & Venus Oriente, Tulum; d incl breakfast US$77; P ⊖ ❋ 🛜) Appealing, Italian-run Tulum hotel with convenient beach and ruins access.

Best Top End

Hotel El Rey del Caribe

(📞 998-884-20-28; www.elreydelcaribe.com; Av Uxmal 24, Cancún Centro; r incl breakfast from US$90; ⊖ ❋ 🛜 ☒; 🚭 R-1) Ecofriendly hotel near the trendy Avenida Náder restaurant/bar zone.

Le Blanc

(📞 998-881-47-48, 800-462-07-92, US 800-986-5632; www.leblancsparesort.com; Blvd Kukulcán Km 10, Zona

Hotelera; d/ste all-inclusive from US$793/868; P ⊖ ❋ 🛜 ☒; 🚭 R-1, R-2) Adults-only resort with amenities that put the other Zona Hotelera hotels to shame.

Beachscape Kin Ha Villas & Suites

(📞 998-891-54-00; www.beachscape.com.mx; Blvd Kukulcán Km 8.5, Zona Hotelera; d/ste incl breakfast from US$156/185; P ⊖ ❋ @ 🛜 ☒; 🚭 R-1) Tranquil resort on a pretty beach with swimmable waters.

La Posada del Sol

(📞 cell 984-1348874; www.laposadadelsol.com; Carretera Tulum-Boca Paila Km 3.5. Tulum; r incl breakfast US$100 190; ⊖ 🛜) Stands out for creative architecture and natural design details such as recycled objects found after a hurricane.

Casa Sirena

(📞 cell 998-2425906; www.casasirenamexico.com; Hidalgo s/n, Isla Mujeres; r incl breakfast from US$208, ⊖ ❋ 🛜 ☒) Lovingly restored, adults-only, historic house, with six elegant rooms and a sea-view balcony.

Rancho Encantado

(📞 998-884-20-71; www.

encantado.com; Hwy 307 Km 24, Laguna Bacalar; d/ste incl breakfast from $2637/3007; ⓟ🏊❄🛜📺) The most enchanting stay at dreamy Laguna Bacalar, featuring immaculate cabins and jacuzzis.

Arriving in Cancún & the Riviera Maya

Aeropuerto Internacional de Cancún

○ The area's only international airport is Cancún (CUN), about 8km south of downtown.

○ It has all the services you would expect from a major international airport: ATMs, money exchange and car-rental agencies.

○ It's served by many direct international flights and by connecting flights from Mexico City. Low-cost Mexican carriers VivaAerobus, Interjet

and Volaris have services from Mexico City.

○ Frequent buses (M$82, 25 minutes) depart from the airport terminals to the bus station in Cancún Centro. For the Zona Hotelera, it's best to take an airport shuttle van (shared M$180, nonstop M$1100) or taxi M$650 to your hotel.

ADO Bus Station

○ Buses arrive in **Cancún Centro** (www. ado.com.mx; cnr Avs Uxmal & Tulum), where you can catch a bus or a taxi to your hotel, or walk if you're staying near the downtown terminal.

○ Taxis waiting outside the bus station charge about M$150 to M$200 to the Zona Hotelera; buses (M$12) to the hotel zone run along Avenida Tulum, adjacent to the ADO station.

Cozumel International Airport

○ Shared shuttles from the airport into town cost about M$70. For hotels on the island's north and south ends, they charge M$150 to M$200.

Getting Around

Bicycle

○ Bicycling is becoming a more common mode of transportation in some cities.

○ Never assume that motorists will give you the right of way and be particularly careful on narrow roads.

○ You can rent bikes in many towns for about M$30/100 per hour/day.

Bus

○ 1st- and 2nd-class buses go pretty much everywhere in the region.

○ Most cities and towns have one main bus terminal where all long-distance buses arrive and depart.

○ **Grupo ADO** (☎5784-4652; www.ado.com.mx); operates many of the bus lines that you'll be using.

Car & Motorcycle

○ Great option for traveling outside big cities.

o Expect to pay about M$750 a day for rental and gas.

o Drivers should ideally know some Spanish, have reserves of patience and access to extra cash for emergencies.

o Motorcycling around the Yucatán is not for the fainthearted. Roads and traffic can be rough, and parts and mechanics hard to come by.

Ferry

o Frequent boats depart from Playa del Carmen to Cozumel, Chiquilá to Isla Holbox and Cancún to Isla Mujeres.

o For information about schedules, points of departure and car ferries, see www.granpuerto. com.mx and www. transcaribe.net.

Taxi

o Taxis are common in towns and cities, and surprisingly economical. City rides usually cost around M$25 to M$30 for a short trip.

o If there's no meter, which is usually the case, agree on a price before getting in the cab.

o Renting a taxi for a day-long, out-of-town jaunt generally costs something similar to a rental car by the time you're done with gas – M$750 to M$1000.

Shared Van

o On much of the peninsula, a variety of vehicles – often Volkswagen, Ford or Chevrolet vans – operate shared transportation services between towns or nearby neighborhoods.

o These vehicles usually leave whenever they are full.

o Fares are typically less than those of 1st-class buses. Combi is a term often used for the Volkswagen variety; colectivo refers to any van type. Taxi colectivo may mean either public or private transport, depending on the location.

Essential Information

Accessible Travel

o Lodgings on the Yucatán Peninsula generally don't cater for travelers with disabilities, though some hotels and restaurants (mostly toward the top end of the market) and some public buildings now provide wheelchair access.

o Mobility is easiest in the major tourist resorts. Bus transportation can be difficult; flying or taking a taxi is easier.

o Lodgings in Cancún generally do not cater to travelers with disabilities, however, you'll have a better chance of finding hotels and restaurants with wheelchair access in the Zona Hotelera.

o The visually impaired will find it difficult to get around on Cancún's busy streets.

Business Hours

Where there are significant seasonal variations in opening hours, we provide hours for high season. Some hours may be shorter in shoulder and low seasons. Hours vary widely but the following are fairly typical.

Banks 9am to 4pm Monday to Friday, 9am to 1pm Saturday

Restaurants 9am to 11pm

Cafes 8am to 10pm

Bars and clubs 1pm to midnight

Shops 9am to 8pm Monday to Saturday (supermarkets and department stores 9am to 10pm daily)

Discount Cards

Discount cards can get you reduced airfare at youth-oriented travel agencies and occasionally they'll get you discounted prices at museums and archaeological sites. Seniors over 60 get free admission into the Museo Maya de Cancún (p52) with proof of ID.

ISIC student card

IYTC (under 26 years) card

ITIC card for teachers

Electricity

Type A
120V/60Hz

Type B
120V/60Hz

Emergencies

Country code	☏ 52
Emergency	☏ 911
International access code	☏ 00
National tourist assistance (including emergencies)	☏ 088

Insurance

A travel-insurance policy to cover theft, loss and medical problems is a good idea. Some policies specifically exclude dangerous activities such as scuba diving and motorcycling.

LGBTIQ Travelers

Same-sex marriage is legal in Quintana Roo and Cancún is considered to be one of the state's most progressive cities. Gay Cities website (http://cancun.gaycities.com) lists bars and gay-friendly hotels in Cancún and www.gaymexicomap.com has some good recommendations as well. Most locals have open-minded views about sexuality and gays and lesbians rarely attract open discrimination and violence.

The **11:11** (p46) nightclub makes a good starting point to tap into the LGBTIQ scene.

Money

Mexico's currency is the peso (M$). Mexico is largely a cash economy. ATMs and exchange offices are widely available. Credit cards are accepted in many midrange and top-end hotels, restaurants and stores.

ATMs

ATMs (caja permanente or cajero automático) are plentiful and are the easiest source of cash, though a few tourist areas still remain without. You can use major credit cards and some bank cards, such as those on the Cirrus and Plus systems, to withdraw pesos (or dollars) from ATMs. The exchange rate that banks use for ATM withdrawals is normally better than the 'tourist rate' – though that advantage is negated by transaction fees and other methods that banks have of taking your money.

Bargaining

It's worth asking if a discount is available on room rates, especially if it's low season or you're staying more than two nights. In markets some haggling is expected. Unmetered taxis will often shave some pesos off the initial asking price.

Changing Money

You can change currency in banks or at casas de cambio (money-exchange offices). Banks have longer lines than casas de cambio and usually shorter hours. Casas de cambio can easily be found in just about every large or medium-size town and in some smaller ones. Some exchange offices will ask for your passport as a form of ID.

Public Holidays

Día de Muertos (Day of the Dead) on November 1 and 2 is considered an optional holiday.

Año Nuevo (New Year's Day) January 1

Día de la Constitución (Constitution Day) February 5

Tipping

Hotels About 5% to 10% of room costs for staff.

Restaurants 15% if service is not included in the check.

Supermarket baggers/gas-station attendants Usually around M$5.

Porters M$25 per bag.

Taxis Drivers don't expect tips unless they provide an extra service.

Bars Bartenders usually don't get tipped, so anything is appreciated.

Dos & Don'ts

Greetings A handshake is standard when meeting people for the first time. Among friends, men usually exchange back-slapping hugs; for women it's usually a kiss on the cheek.

Conversation Yucatecans are generally warm and entertaining conversationalists. As a rule, they express disagreement more by nuance than by open contradiction. The Maya can be slightly more reserved in conversation.

Getting directions Mexicans are very cordial and eager to please, so much so that some folks will steer you in the wrong direction rather than saying they don't know where a particular place is. It can be frustrating at times, but keep in mind that it's done with good intentions.

Día del Nacimiento de Benito Juárez
(Benito Juárez's birthday) March 21

Día del Trabajo (Labor Day) May 1

Día de la Independencia (Independence Day) September 16

Día de la Revolución (Revolution Day) November 20

Día de Navidad (Christmas Day) December 25

Safe Travel

o Despite all the grim news about Mexico's drug-related violence, the Yucatán Peninsula remains relatively safe for those not engaged in illegal activities.

o Most of the killings you hear about happen between rival drug gangs, so tourists are rarely caught up in the disputes.

o Cancún, Playa del Carmen and Tulum have all seen a gradual rise in drug violence, but major US cities such as New York and Chicago have higher murder rates than the entire state of Yucatán.

o The biggest danger in Cancún isn't violent crime – it's the streets themselves. Vehicles speed along narrow roads and pedestrians (often drunk) sometimes get injured.

o A poked eye or twisted ankle is more common than a shooting or mugging; however, if anyone *does* demand money, don't argue. Most violent incidents involve fights where tourists put themselves in danger.

o Do not purchase drugs on the street or be seen talking to street dealers: this can be interpreted by either police or gangs as you being involved, marking you for interrogation or mugging.

Telephone Services

Many US cell-phone companies offer Mexico roaming deals. Local SIM cards can only be used in phones that have been unlocked.

Toilets

Public toilets are rare, so take advantage of facilities in places such as hotels, restaurants, bus terminals and museums; a fee of about M$5 may be charged. It's fairly common for toilets in budget hotels and restaurants to lack seats.

When out and about, carry some toilet paper with you because it often won't be provided. If there's a bin beside the toilet (nearly always, except in ritzy hotels), put soiled paper in it because the drains can't cope otherwise.

Tourist Information

Just about every town of interest to tourists along the Riviera Maya has a state or municipal tourist office. They are generally helpful with maps, brochures and questions, and often some staff members speak English.

Amigos de Isla Contoy (☎ 998-884-74-83; www. facebook.com/amigosde

islacontoyac; Local 1, 2nd fl, Plaza Bonita Mall, Cancún Centro; ☺ 9am-5pm Mon-Fri) Has helpful info about Isla Contoy and works to conserve the island.

Cancún Visitors Bureau (cancun.travel/en) An informative website, but no tourist office.

Casa Consular (Map p54; D4; ☎ 998-840-60-82, cell 998-2409545; www.casaconsular.org; Blvd Kukulcán Km 13, Zona Hotelera; ☺ 9am-5pm Mon-Fri, to 1pm Sat) While it doesn't provide consular assistance, Casa Consular will find the exact information you need and tell you where you need to go. It is a service for all visitors, not just those with an embassy or consulate in the city. Located inside the police and fire department building.

City Tourism Office (Map p38, E4; ☎ 998-887-33-79; www.facebook.com/direcciongeneralde

turismo; cnr Avs Cobá & Náder, Cancún Centro; ☺ 9am-4pm Mon-Fri) City tourist office with ample supplies of printed material and knowledgeable staff.

Visas

Every tourist must have a Mexican-government tourist permit, easily obtained on arrival. Citizens of the US, Canada, EU countries, Argentina, Australia, Brazil, Israel, Japan, New Zealand, Norway and Switzerland are among those who do not need visas to enter Mexico as tourists. Chinese, Indians, Russians and South Africans are among those who do need a visa. But Mexican visas are not required for people of any nationality who hold a valid US, Canadian or Schengen visa.

Language

Although the predominant language of Mexico is Spanish, about 50 indigenous languages are spoken as a first language by more than seven million people throughout the country.

Mexican Spanish pronunciation is easy, as most sounds have equivalents in English. Note that *kh* is a throaty sound (like the 'ch' in the Scottish *loch*), *v* and *b* are both pronounced like a soft English 'v' (between a 'v' and a 'b'), and *r* is strongly rolled. Also keep in mind that in some parts of Mexico the letters *ll* and *y* are pronounced like the 'll' in 'million', but in most areas they are pronounced like the 'y' in 'yes,' and this is how they are represented in our pronunciation guides. The stressed syllables are indicated with italics.

To enhance your trip with a phrasebook, visit lonelyplanet.com.

Basics

Hello.	*Hola.*	o·la
Goodbye.	*Adiós.*	a·dyos
How are you?	*¿Qué tal?*	ke tal
Fine, thanks.	*Bien, gracias,*	byen gra·syas
Excuse me.	*Perdón.*	per·don
Sorry.	*Lo siento.*	lo syen·to
Please.	*Por favor.*	por fa·vor
Thank you.	*Gracias.*	gra·syas
You're welcome.	*De nada.*	de na·da
Yes./No.	*Sí./No.*	see/no

My name is ...
Me llamo ...   me ya·mo ...

What's your name?
¿Cómo se llama usted?   ko·mo se ya·ma oo·ste (pol)
¿Cómo te llamas?   ko·mo te ya·mas (inf)

Do you speak English?
¿Habla inglés?   a·bla een·gles (pol)
¿Hablas inglés?   a·blas een·gles (inf)

I don't understand.
Yo no entiendo.   yo no en·tyen·do

Eating & Drinking

Can I see the menu, please?
¿Puedo ver el menú, por favor?   pwe·do ver el me·noo por fa·vor

What would you recommend?
¿Qué recomienda?   ke re·ko·myen·da

I don't eat (meat).
No como (carne).   no ko·mo (kar·ne)

That was delicious!
¡Estaba buenísimo!   es·ta·ba bwe·nee·see·mo

Cheers!
¡Salud!   sa·loo

The bill, please.
La cuenta, por favor.   la kwen·ta por fa·vor

Shopping

I'd like to buy ...
Quisiera kee·sye·ra
comprar ... kom·prar...

I'm just looking.
Sólo estoy so·lo es·toy
mirando. mee·ran·do

Can I look at it?
¿Puedo verlo? pwe·do ver·lo

How much is it?
¿Cuánto cuesta? kwan·to kwes·ta

Emergencies

Help!	¡Socorro!	so·ko·ro
Go away!	¡Vete!	ve·te
Call ...!	¡Llame a ...!	ya·me a ...
a doctor	un médico	oon me·dee·ko
the police	la policía	la po·lee·see·a

I'm lost.
Estoy es·toy
perdido/a. per·dee·do/a (m/f)

Where are the toilets?
¿Dónde están los don·de es·tan los
baños? ba·nyos

I'm ill.
Estoy es·toy
enfermo/a. en·fer·mo/a (m/f)

Time & Numbers

What time is it?
¿Qué hora es? ke o·ra es

It's (10) o'clock.
Son (las diez). son (las dyes)

It's half past (one).
Es (la una) es (la oo·na)
y media. ee me·dya

Transport & Directions

boat	barco	bar·ko
bus	autobús	ow·to·boos
plane	avión	a·vyon
train	tren	tren

A ... ticket, please.
Un billete oon bee·ye·te
de ..., por favor. de ... por fa·vor

1st-class
primera pree·me·ra
clase kla·se

2nd-class
segunda se·goon·da
clase kla·se

one-way *ida* ee·da

return *ida y* ee·da ee
vuelta vwel·ta

What time does it arrive/leave?
¿A qué hora a ke o·ra
llega/sale? ye·ga/sa·le

Does it stop at ...?
¿Para en ...? pa·ra en ...

What stop is this?
¿Cuál es kwal es es·ta
esta parada? pa·ra·da

Please tell me when we get to ...
¿Puede pwe·de
avisarme a·vee·sar·me
cuando kwan·do
lleguemos a ...? ye·ge·mos a ...

I want to get off here.
Quiero bajarme kye·ro ba·khar·me
aquí. a·kee

Behind the Scenes

Send Us Your Feedback

We love to hear from travelers – your comments help make our books better. We read every word, and we guarantee that your feedback goes straight to the authors. Visit **lonelyplanet.com/contact** to submit your updates and suggestions.

Note: We may edit, reproduce and incorporate your comments in Lonely Planet products such as guidebooks, websites and digital products, so let us know if you don't want your comments reproduced or your name acknowledged. For a copy of our privacy policy visit lonelyplanet.com/privacy.

John's Thanks

Very special thanks to Jesus Navarrete, Ursula Reischl, Chicken Willy, destination editor Sarah Stocking, co-author Ray Bartlett and to all the *quintanarooenses* for their generous support and the good times. As always, my heartfelt gratitude to Lau for taking care of the kitties and everything else.

Ray's Thanks

Thanks first and always to my family and friends, for letting me go on these adventures and still remembering me when I get back, or for joining me whenever possible. Huge thanks to Sarah Stocking for the editorial wisdom and advice extraordinaire, to my co-author John, and the rest of the LP staff. To all people I met or who helped me along the way, especially Naomi, Vivian, Odile, Ale, Eziquiel, Fabiola, Selena, Yuli, Alex, and so many others. Thanks so much. Can't wait to be back again soon.

Acknowledgements

Cover photograph: Xcaret, Riviera Maya, Degree/4Corners ©

This Book

This 1st edition of Lonely Planet's *Cancún & the Riviera Maya* guidebook was researched and written by Ashley Harrell, Ray Bartlett, John Hecht and Laura Winfree. This guidebook was produced by the following:

Destination Editor
Sarah Stocking

Senior Product Editors
Vicky Smith, Martine Power

Regional Senior Cartographer Corey Hutchison

Product Editor Grace Dobell

Book Designer
Virginia Moreno

Assisting Editors
Judith Bamber, Carolyn Boicos, Samantha Cook,
Andrea Dobbin, Allison Morris, Lauren O'Connell, Charlotte Orr

Assisting Book Designers
Brooke Giacomin, Aomi Ito

Cover Researcher
Brendan Dempsey-Spencer

Thanks to Kirsten Rawlings, Ross Taylor

Index

See also separate subindexes for:

🟦 **Eating p157**
🟦 **Drinking p157**
🟦 **Entertainment p158**
🟦 **Shopping p158**

Index

Sights 000
Map Pages **000**